Editor:
Charles Payne

Editor in Chief:
Sharon Coan, M.S. Ed.

Art Director:
Elayne Roberts

Art Coordination Assistant:
Cheri Macourbrie Wilson

Cover Artist:
Tina DeLeon

Product Manager:
Phil Garcia

Imaging:
Phil Garcia

Publishers:
Rachelle Cracchiolo, M.S. Ed.
Mary Dupuy Smith, M.S. Ed.

INTERNET ACTIVITIES FOR MATH

CHALLENGING

Author:

Walter Sherwood

Teacher Created Materials, Inc.
6421 Industry Way
Westminster, CA   92683
ISBN-1-57690-193-9

©*1998 Teacher Created Materials, Inc.*   Made in U.S.A.

TABLE OF CONTENTS

INTRODUCTION

Use the 25 classroom-ready lesson plans and student activities in this book to tap into the Internet and make your classroom come alive. Imagine the students' interest as they calculate what the national debt will be when they graduate from high school using up-to-date, current data. Or, have them investigate the degree of accuracy of weather forecasts using real-time data from cities across the country. The possibilities are endless. As you use the activities, keep in mind several things.

First, before using any of the activities, you must familiarize yourself with the use of the Internet. Additionally, you will need to provide instruction for your class on how to use the Internet. This book assumes the teacher and students have a working knowledge of the Internet and understand the basics of conducting searches. Don't panic if you feel like you need to know more about using the Internet; plenty of help is available.

Second, before using any activities, it is strongly recommended you verify the suggested Web sites that you will use in the activities. Web sites frequently change addresses or become unavailable for a myriad of reasons. Again, don't panic; there is almost always an alternate site available that contains similar information, but you may have to search for that site.

Third, in general, the activities can be used for either individual students or small groups. Depending on the availability of computers and the needs of your students, you may decide on how to arrange for student participation. Additionally, some of the information gathered from the activities can be used at home where students might have access to the Internet.

Finally, it is suggested that you begin with the activity "Internet Scavenger Hunt," which will sharpen the students' data gathering skills. Enjoy this new and exciting world of learning and watch as your students become more motivated and excited about mathematics.

INTERNET SCAVENGER HUNT

Teacher Notes

NCTM Standards, Grades 5–8: Problem Solving, Communication, Connections, Number Relationships, and Statistics.

Objectives:

Students will...

- search for answers to questions using the Internet.
- keep a record of how long each search took, the terms searched for, and the different sites visited to get to their answers.
- record the Uniform Resource Locator (URL) or Web site address where they found their answer.
- calculate mean, median, mode, and range for their times and the class's times.
- display their data on poster paper.

Materials Needed:

- Computer with Internet access
- Poster paper
- Stopwatches

Web Sites:

- Any search engine will work for this investigation.

Time: approximately 3–4 hours

Teaching the Lesson:

- It is important that students accurately record how long each search took since they will analyze this data when they finish their searches.
- The intent of keeping track of times is not to have students race but rather to investigate how long it takes to find information.
- There may be more than one site where students will be able to find answers to the questions.
- Stress the importance of accurately recording the URL of the site where they get their answers because even a small error will make it difficult to verify their answers.

Selected Answers:

Some possible answers include

Search One:	http://tigerx.com/trivia/tallest.htm
Search Two:	http://www.inch.com/~dipper/world.html
Search Three:	http://www.billboard-online.com
Search Six:	http://Freeway.net/~michaels/topmovie.html

INTERNET SCAVENGER HUNT

Student Activity Sheet

Name: _____

Date: _____ Per: _____

Have you ever gone on a scavenger hunt? It can be fun and challenging. This scavenger hunt uses the Internet. You don't have to get out of your chair, but you are sure to travel far, so hold on and good luck finding your answers!

When you are searching for your answers, keep an accurate record of how long (in seconds) it takes you to locate the answer.   Also, write down all the sites you visit in searching for your answer and the Uniform Resource Locator (URL) or Web site address of where you find the answer to the question. When you describe how you found your answer, you should list the actual steps you followed to find your answer by listing what you searched for and the sites you visited.   When you have completed all of your searches, you will compile and analyze your data and the data for the entire class.

Search Number One:

Who is the governor of your state? List the governor's name and when his or her term of office began.

Start time:_____ Stop time:_____ Total time: _____

Governor's Name: _____

Began Term: _____

1. What is the URL of the site where you found your answer?

   _____

2. Document the steps you followed to find your answer.

   _____

   _____

INTERNET SCAVENGER HUNT *(cont.)*

Search Number Two:

What are the five tallest buildings in the world? List their names, where they are located, their heights, and the year they were built.

Start time:_____   Stop time: _____   Total time: _____

	Building Name	Location	Height	Year Built
1.				
2.				
3.				
4.				
5.				

1. What is the URL where you found your answer?

_____

2. Document the steps you followed to find your answer. _____

_____

_____

INTERNET SCAVENGER HUNT *(cont.)*

Search Number Three:

What are the five highest mountains in the world? Record their names, where they are located, and their heights.

Start time:_____ Stop time: _____ Total time: _____

	Mountain Name	Location	Height
1.			
2.			
3.			
4.			
5.			

1. What is the URL of the site where you found your answer?

_____

2. Document the steps you followed to find your answer. _____

_____

_____

INTERNET SCAVENGER HUNT *(cont.)*

Search Number Four:

What are the five longest rivers in the world? List their names, where they are located, and their lengths.

Start time:_____ Stop time:_____ Total time: _____

	River Name	Location	Length
1.			
2.			
3.			
4.			
5.			

1. What is the URL of the site where you found your answer?

_____

2. Document the steps you followed to find your answer.

_____

_____

INTERNET SCAVENGER HUNT *(cont.)*

Search Number Five:

What were the five top grossing movies last week? List the names of the movies and the amount of money they earned last week.

Start time:_____   Stop time:_____   Total time: _____

	Movie	Amount Earned
1.		
2.		
3.		
4.		
5.		

1. What is the URL of the site where you found your answer?

_____

2. Document the steps you followed to find your answer. _____

_____

_____

INTERNET SCAVENGER HUNT *(cont.)*

Search Number Six:

What are the top five country albums on the Billboard chart? List the artist(s), titles, and how long each has been on the chart.

Start time:_____ Stop time:_____ Total time: _____

	Artist(s)	Title	Weeks on the Chart
1.			
2.			
3.			
4.			
5.			

1. What is the URL where you found your answer?

_____

2. Document the steps you followed to find your answer. _____

_____

_____

INTERNET SCAVENGER HUNT *(cont.)*

Analyze Your Data

In the table, record the time it took to find each answer.

Total Searching Times

Question	1	2	3	4	5	6	Total
Time							

Calculate the mean, median, mode, and range for your times.

Mean: _____

Median: _____

Mode: _____

Range: _____

Analyze the Class Data

Now collect the data from the rest of the class in the table below. On the next page, calculate the mean, median, mode, and range for the entire class.

Individual Times for All Students

Mean	
Median	
Mode	
Range	

INTERNET SCAVENGER HUNT *(cont.)*

Class Mean:_____

Class Median: _____

Class Mode:_____

Class Range: _____

1. What was the difference between the class's average measurements and yours?

   _____

   _____

2. Which search was the most difficult for you? Explain why.

   _____

   _____

   _____

   _____

3. Based on the data for the entire class, which search was the most difficult for the class? Explain why.

   _____

   _____

   _____

   _____

4. On a piece of poster paper, construct a graph to display both the class data and your own data.

Design Your Own Internet Scavenger Hunt

Challenge your classmates by designing your own Internet scavenger hunt. It can be as easy or difficult as you would like. Decide on the questions and the type of information that will be searched for. Write out your questions and give them to someone else in your class. Remember, though, you have to be able to answer the questions too.

EXPLORING THE SOLAR SYSTEM

Teacher Notes

NCTM Standards, Grades 5–8: Problem Solving, Number Relationships, Computation, Estimation, and Measurement.

Objectives:

Students will...

- use the Internet to gather data about the physical and orbital properties of the planets in the solar system.
- make metric unit conversions and make conversions between metric units and customary units.
- convert between scientific notation and standard notation and vice versa.
- construct tables and graphs.
- draw conclusions and make predictions based on their data.
- construct a mathematically accurate model of the solar system.

Materials Needed:

- Computer with Internet access
- Scientific or graphing calculator
- Metric ruler or meterstick
- Poster paper

Web Sites:

- http://www.seds.org/nineplanets/nineplanets/
- http://bang.lanl.gov/solarsys/homepage.htm
- http://www.ast.cam.ac.uk/pubinfo/leaflets/solar_system/section3.2.html
- http://www.execpc.com/~wallin/convert
- http://www.mplik.ru/~sg/transl/index.html (your browser must be *Java* capable)

Time: approximately 3–4 hours

Teaching the Lesson:

- Students will need a review on scientific notation concepts and how to enter numbers in scientific notation into their calculators.
- Before the students complete the physical and orbital data tables, demonstrate how to perform the conversions for one planet.
- If students are having trouble scaling down planet size, suggest a centimeter scale of 1:1 billion.
- Students will discover that the planet distances for a 1:1 billion cm scale model will not fit on a piece of poster paper. Help them experiment with different distance scales so that they can fit the solar system on their papers.
- When students are exploring the relationship between distance from the sun and period, they will need to draw a scatter plot. Since the distances and periods vary so greatly, have students draw the four closest planets to the sun on one plot and the other five planets on a separate plot.

EXPLORING THE SOLAR SYSTEM

Student Activity Sheet

Name: _____

Date: _____ Per: _____

Andy, the wannabe astronomer, needs your help in constructing a scale model drawing of the solar system. Complete the following steps to show him how it is done.

Physical Data

Complete the following table of physical data of the planets. Locate the data at one of these suggested Web sites:

- http://www.seds.org/nineplanets/nineplanets/
- http://bang.lanl.gov/solarsys/homepage.htm
- http://www.ast.cam.ac.uk/pubinfo/leaflets/solar_system/section3.2.html

Or search for another Web site about planets using this site:

- http://www.yahoo.com/Science/Astronomy/

Table One: Physical Data of the Planets

Planet	Radius (km)	Radius (miles)	Radius (in scientific notation—cm)	Diameter (km)

EXPLORING THE SOLAR SYSTEM *(cont.)*

For hints on how to convert between kilometers and centimeters and between kilometers and miles, visit one of these Web sites:

- http://www.execpc.com/~wallin/convert
- http://www.mplik.ru/~sg/transl/index.html (your browser must be *Java* capable)

Orbital Data

Complete the table below for orbital data.

Table Two: Orbital Data for the Planets

Planet	Distance from Sun (km)	Distance from Sun (miles)	Distance from Sun (in scientific notation—cm)	Period (days)	Period (years)

Scale Models

With the data you collected, help Andy make a scale model drawing of the solar system.

EXPLORING THE SOLAR SYSTEM *(cont.)*

1. First, you have to decide on your conversion factor. Ask yourself what factor you need to reduce the data by so that it will fit on poster board. Experiment with some different values for scales now.

_____

_____

_____

If you are still having trouble, see your teacher for some suggestions. After you have chosen your conversion factor, fill in the table below to help scale down your data before you draw your solar system.

Table Three: Conversion Table

Planet	Actual Diameter (km)	Scale____ Size in cm	Actual Distance from the sun (km)	Scale____ Distance in cm

EXPLORING THE SOLAR SYSTEM *(cont.)*

2. After completing your table, what suggestions do you have for Andy so that he can make his scale model of the solar system fit onto a piece of poster paper?

_____

_____

3. After you have calculated the dimensions for your drawing, construct an accurate model on poster paper. Be sure to label each planet and indicate the scales you are using for size and distance.

Further Explorations

1. After completing his table and making his scale drawing (with your expert help), Andy was feeling pretty good about his chances of becoming an astronomer. In fact, he was sure he would be the one to discover a planet past Pluto. In order to help him narrow his search, he needs to know about how far from the sun the planet would be and what its approximate period would be. Construct two scatter plots that show the period versus distance and make a prediction of the distance and period of Andy's planet. Use the first scatter plot for the four planets closest to the sun. Use the second scatter plot for the next five planets.

EXPLORING THE SOLAR SYSTEM *(cont.)*

2. Describe the relationship between the distance and the period.

_____

_____

_____

3. If a 10th planet was discovered past Pluto, how far from the sun would it be? What would you expect its period to be? Explain.

_____

_____

_____

_____

_____

SIZE IS RELATIVE

Teacher Notes

NCTM Standards, Grades 5–8: Problem Solving, Reasoning, Connections, Number Relationships, Computation, Estimation, and Measurement.

Objectives:

Students will...

- measure their heights and covert them to feet, centimeters, and meters.
- use the Internet to find the heights of the Washington Monument, the highest point in their state, and the depth of the Marianas Trench.
- set up proportions comparing their heights to the heights of the Washington Monument, the highest point in their state, and the depth of the Marianas Trench.
- calculate the decimal, fraction, and percent equivalents for each ratio.
- make a scale drawing that will include themselves, the Washington Monument, the highest point in their state, and the Marianas Trench.

Materials Needed:

- Computer with Internet access
- Calculators
- Tape measure
- Rulers or metersticks
- Poster paper

Web Sites:

- http://www.execpc.com/~wallip/convert
- http://www.mplik.ru/~sg/transl/index.html (must be *Java* capable)
- http://www.nps.gov/wamo/index2.htm
- http:// www.inch.com/~dipper/highpoints.html
- http://www.whoi.edu/general/deepest-ocean.html
- http://www.ocean.washington.edu/exploraquarium/faq.htm

Time: approximately 2–3 hours

Teaching the Lesson:

- Have students record their heights in feet by using decimals. You may need to demonstrate how to convert from fractions to decimals.
- The Washington Monument is a suggested comparison. If there is a more familiar landmark or building in your city, then use it.
- Some students will recognize the pattern that is developing in the tables; if they do not, ask questions to lead students in that direction.
- Students will need to experiment with scales for their drawings. Remind them that they will be including other objects that might be much taller or deeper.
- Some students may choose to use the depth of the Marianas Trench as a negative number.

Selected Answers:

- Washington Monument: 555 feet high
- Marianas Trench: 11,020 meters deep

SIZE IS RELATIVE

Student Activity Sheet

Name: _____

Date: _____ Per: _____

Have you ever stood at the bottom of a very tall building and wondered just how tall it was? Think for a moment about the tallest building or the highest mountain you have ever seen. Sometimes it is hard to relate to their massive heights. By comparing a known height, for instance, to how tall you are, you will be better able to understand the relationship between heights of different objects.

How Tall Are You?

A good place to begin your understanding of the height of something is to measure your own height. Work in pairs to measure your heights. Record your height below. Then list your height in inches, feet, centimeters, and meters. For a conversion table go to

- http://www.execpc.com/~wallip/convert
- http://www.mplik.ru/~sg/transl/index.html (Your browser must be *Java* capable.)

Your height in inches: _____

Your height in feet (use decimals): _____

Your height in centimeters: _____

Your height in meters (use decimals): _____

Washington Monument

Let's see how you compare to the Washington Monument. Go to the Web site below and find out the height of the Washington Monument. List its height in inches, feet, centimeters, and meters.

- http://www.nps.gov/wamo/index2.htm

Washington Monument height in inches:_____

SIZE IS RELATIVE *(cont.)*

Washington Monument height in feet:_____

Washington Monument height in centimeters: _____

Washington Monument height in meters: _____

How Do You Stack Up?

1. Compare your height to the Washington Monument's height by setting up a ratio in inches, feet, centimeters, and meters. Express your answers as fractions, decimals, and percents. Fill in the table with your values.

Inches	Fraction	Decimal	Percent
Your Height ⎯⎯⎯ Washington Monument			

Feet	Fraction	Decimal	Percent
Your Height ⎯⎯⎯ Washington Monument			

Centimeters	Fraction	Decimal	Percent
Your Height ⎯⎯⎯ Washington Monument			

SIZE IS RELATIVE *(cont.)*

Meters	Fraction	Decimal	Percent
Your Height ——————— Washington Monument			

2. What conclusions or observations can you make about your height in comparison to the height of the Washington Monument. Explain.

_____

_____

_____

Scale Drawing

On a piece of poster paper, make a scale drawing of your height and the height of the Washington Monument. Leave enough room for two more scale drawings.

The High Point of the Lesson

1. Now let's see how you compare to the highest point in your state. Visit the Web site below and follow the links to find the highest point in your state. Record its height in inches, feet, centimeters, and meters.

   • http:// www.inch.com/~dipper/highpoints.html

The highest point in my state is_____

Inches	Fraction	Decimal	Percent
Your Height ——————— Highest Point			

SIZE IS RELATIVE *(cont.)*

2. Before you complete the rest of the ratios in the table, make a prediction about what they will be. Explain.

_____

_____

_____

Now complete the rest of the tables.

Feet	Fraction	Decimal	Percent
Your Height ⁄ Highest Point			

Centimeters	Fraction	Decimal	Percent
Your Height ⁄ Highest Point			

Meters	Fraction	Decimal	Percent
Your Height ⁄ Highest Point			

3. Add your state's highest point to your scale drawing. Leave room for one more addition to the drawing.

SIZE IS RELATIVE *(cont.)*

How Deep Is It?

1. This time you are going to compare heights with the deepest point in the world. Where do you think the deepest point in the world is located? For those of you who guessed under water, you're right. In fact, the name of the deepest spot on earth is the Marianas Trench. Go to the Web site below and find out the depth of the Marianas Trench.

    *   http://www.whoi.edu/general/deepest-ocean.html

Marianas Trench depth in inches: _____

Marianas Trench depth in feet: _____

Marianas Trench depth in centimeters: _____

Marianas Trench depth in meters:_____

2. If you were going to fill up the Marianas Trench with duplicates of the Washington Monument, how many monuments would you need to stack on top of each other? Explain.

    _____

    _____

    _____

3. What is the ratio of the highest point in your state to the Marianas Trench? Also include the decimal and percent equivalents.

    _____

    _____

    _____

4. Explain how you would estimate how many people standing head to toe would be needed to fill up the Marianas Trench.

    _____

    _____

    _____

5. Complete your scale drawing by adding to it the Marianas Trench. Look back over your drawing and add any additional information such as scales, labels, or legends.

PRIME TIME

Teacher Notes

NCTM Standards, Grades 5–8: Problem Solving, Communication, Reasoning, Connections, Number Relationships, Computation, and Measurement.

Objectives:

Students will...

- use the Internet to define math vocabulary words associated with prime numbers.
- visit the "Largest Known Prime Number" home page to learn more about prime numbers.
- make investigations using the largest known prime number.

Materials Needed:

- Computer with Internet access
- Calculator
- Stopwatch

Web Sites:

- http://www.mathpro.com/math/glossary/glossary.html
- http://www.gps.caltech.edu/~eww/math/math.html
- http://www.utm.edu/research/primes/largest.html
- http://math.rice.edu/~ddonovan/Lessons/eratos.html

Time: approximately 2 hours

Teaching the Lesson:

- You may wish to familiarize yourself with the "Largest Known Prime Number" home page prior to using this lesson.
- Students may confuse the concept of how many digits a number contains with the quantity it represents. You will need to explain to your students the difference between these two concepts.
- You will need to review how to convert measurements into the different units.
- You will need to review how to set up a proportion from test data.

Selected Answers:

1. Method for finding very small primes
2. 13 November 1996
3. 420,921
4. Euclid

PRIME TIME

Student Activity Sheet

Name: _____

Date: _____ Per: _____

I am sure you have heard the term prime number before. But how much do you really know about these amazing numbers? They have quite a few unusual characteristics. For instance, did you know that over 2,000 years ago Greek mathematicians proved that there are an infinite number of primes, but until the invention of computers very large primes were never identified? Pretty amazing, huh? The investigation below will help you learn more about the world of prime numbers.

Definitions

Define the following terms using one of the following online dictionaries:

- http://www.mathpro.com/math/glossary/glossary.html
- http://www.gps.caltech.edu/~eww/math/math.html

1. prime number: _____

   _____

2. integer: _____

   _____

3. infinite: _____

   _____

4. divisor: _____

   _____

5. factor: _____

   _____

PRIME TIME *(cont.)*

Visit the Largest Known Prime Number Home Page

Prime numbers have fascinated mathematicians for centuries. Visit the Web page below and learn more about the search for the largest prime numbers and answer the questions that follow.

The Largest Known Primes

- http://www.utm.edu/research/primes/largest.html

1. What is the Sieve of Eratosthenes used for?

   _____

   _____

2. On what date was the largest known prime number discovered?

   _____

3. How many digits does the largest known prime number contain?

   _____

4. What famous mathematician provided a proof for the infinitude of primes?

   _____

More Questions About Primes

1. If you add or subtract using only prime numbers, is the answer always a prime number? Explain.

   _____

   _____

2. When you multiply and divide using only prime numbers, is the result always a prime number? Explain.

   _____

   _____

3. Are all the prime numbers odd? Explain.

   _____

   _____

PRIME TIME *(cont.)*

4. Can a prime number be negative? Explain.

_____

_____

Just How Big Is the Largest Prime Number?

On the "Largest Known Prime Number" Web page is a section that tells you how many digits the largest known prime contains. Use that information to answer the following questions.

1. Suppose you were to write down on a piece of paper all the digits of the largest known prime. List how long it would be in the units given below. The largest known prime is equal to how many

   inches? _____

   football field(s)? _____

   marathon(s)? _____

   centimeters? _____

   10,000 meters races? _____

   school buses? _____

   kilometers? _____

2. How many digits would a number contain that reached all the way around the equator? To find out the measurements of the equator, go to the Web site below.

   • http://math.rice.edu/~ddonovan/Lessons/eratos.html

_____

_____

_____

_____

_____

_____

PRIME TIME *(cont.)*

3. Time how long it takes you to write out a 10–digit number. Set up a proportion and calculate how long it would take you to write the largest known prime.

_____

_____

_____

_____

4. How long would it take to write a number with 1,000,000 digits?

_____

_____

_____

5. Time how long it takes you to say 10 digits out loud. Set up a proportion and calculate how long it would take you to say all the digits in the largest known prime.

_____

_____

_____

_____

6. How long would it take you to count from 1 to 1,000,000 out loud?

_____

_____

_____

WHAT IS THE RELATIONSHIP?

Teacher Notes

NCTM Standards, Grades 5–8: Reasoning, Statistics, Measurement, Patterns, and Functions.

Objectives:

Students will…

- conduct a data gathering investigation in class.
- conduct data gathering investigations on the Internet.
- complete tables and construct scatter plots.
- make predictions based on their data.
- determine if a positive correlation, negative correlation, or no correlation exists with their data.
- design, conduct, and display their own data collecting investigation using the Internet.

Materials Needed:

- Computer with Internet access
- Scientific calculator
- Rulers
- Tape measures
- Grid paper
- Poster paper

Web Sites:

- http://www.utu.fi:80/~jvuorisa/sport/index.html/
- http://www.nationalgeographic.com/ngs/maps/atlas/namerica/usofamm.html
- http://www.census.gov/cgi-bin/gazetteer

Time: approximately 2–3 hours

Teaching the Lesson:

- You may want to review the concepts of positive, negative, and no correlation.
- The data collection exercise for the women's one-mile race should yield a negative correlation.
- The data collection exercise for the men's shot put should yield a positive correlation.
- The data collection exercise for population and latitude should yield no correlation.
- Encourage students to design a research investigation that demonstrates either a positive or negative correlation.
- Review finding lines of best fit prior to using the exercise.

WHAT IS THE RELATIONSHIP?

Student Activity Sheet

Name: _____

Date: _____ Per: _____

Have you ever noticed that tall people tend to have big feet? or the opposite, short people tend to have small feet? The relationship between someone's height and his or her shoe size is easy to see. But, in many instances it can be difficult to look at sets of data and tell whether or not they are related. One way to help you determine their relationship is by using a scatter plot. Below, you will have the opportunity to investigate data by completing tables and constructing scatter plots. Then you will be able to analyze the data and determine if a relationship exists.

Are You As Wide As You Are Long?

1. Working in a small group, take turns measuring the arm span and height of everyone in the group. Record each group member's data in the table below.

Your Group's Height and Arm Span Measurements

Arm Span						
Height						

2. After you have taken all the measurements in your group, collect the data from other groups in the class so that you have the entire class's data.

Height and Arm Span Measurements for the Class

Arm Span										
Height										

Height and Arm Span Measurements for the Class *(cont.)*

Arm Span										
Height										

WHAT IS THE RELATIONSHIP? *(cont.)*

3. Graph the data on the scatter plot below and draw a line of best fit. Be sure to label your graph.

4. If a 7'6" (2.29 m) basketball player visited your class, could you predict his arm span? Explain. What about a 4'8" (1.42 m) gymnast? Explain.

_____

_____

_____

Women's One-Mile Race

1. Visit the Web site below and record the world record time for the women's one-mile race for the years indicated on the next page.

2. After you complete the table, construct a scatter plot from the data. Be sure to choose appropriate scales for your graph and label the y-axis "Time" and the x-axis "Year." Then draw a line of best fit.

- http://www.utu.fi:80/~jvuorisa/sport/index.html/

WHAT IS THE RELATIONSHIP? *(cont.)*

World Record Times for Women's One-Mile Race

Year	1967	1969	1971	1973	1977	1979	1981	1981	1982	1982	1984	1989	1996
Time													

3. Describe the relationship between the winning time and the year.

_____

_____

_____

4. Based on your data, what do you think the winning time will be in the year 2010? Explain.

_____

_____

_____

WHAT IS THE RELATIONSHIP? *(cont.)*

5. Does the data have a positive correlation, negative correlation, or no correlation? Explain.

_____

_____

Men's Shot Put

1. Visit the Web site below and record the world record distance for the men's shot put for the years indicated.

2. After you complete the table, construct a scatter plot from the data. Be sure to choose appropriate scales for your graph and label the y-axis "Distance" and the x-axis "Year." Then draw a line of best fit.

- http://www.utu.fi:80/~jvuorisa/sport/index.htm/

World Record Distances for Men's Shot Put

Year	1967	1969	1971	1973	1977	1979	1981	1981	1982	1982	1984	1989	1996
Distance													

WHAT IS THE RELATIONSHIP? *(cont.)*

3. Describe the relationship between the winning distance and the year.

_____

_____

_____

4. Based on your data, what do you think the winning distance will be in the year 2000? Explain.

_____

_____

5. Does the data have a positive correlation, negative correlation, or no correlation? Explain.

_____

_____

Cities and Their Latitudes

1. Visit Web site (a) below and choose 10 different cities. Then go to Web site (b) and record the current population and latitude for each city you chose. Use the table below and on the next page to record your data. After you complete the tables, construct a scatter plot from the data. Be sure to choose appropriate scales for your graph. Then draw a line of best fit.

   - (a) http://www.nationalgeographic.com/ngs/maps/atlas/namerica/usofamm.html
   - (b) http://www.census.gov/cgi-bin/gazetteer

Population and Latitude

city name					
population					
latitude					

WHAT IS THE RELATIONSHIP? *(cont.)*

city name					
population					
latitude					

2. Describe the relationship between a city's population and latitude.

_____

_____

_____

3. Based on your data, can you predict what the latitude of a city would be if you knew the population? Explain.

_____

_____

_____

WHAT IS THE RELATIONSHIP? *(cont.)*

4. Does the data have a positive correlation, negative correlation, or no correlation? Explain.

_____

_____

Design Your Own Investigation

Design a data collection investigation that determines if a relationship exists between sets of data. In order to collect your data, use the search features on the Internet. Display your data in a table and create a scatter plot. Draw a line of best fit and make a prediction based on your data.

MAYAN MATH

Teacher Notes

NCTM Standards, Grades 5–8: Communication, Connections, and Number Relationships.

Objectives:

Students will...

- use the Internet to explore how the Mayan culture used mathematical symbols.

- use Mayan Math symbols to write and solve problems.

Materials Needed:

- Computer with Internet access

Web Site:

- http://hanksville.phast.umass.edu/yucatan/mayamath.html

Time: approximately 2–3 hours

Teaching the Lesson:

- This lesson can be integrated with applicable social studies lessons.

- Have students read through the "Mayan Math" Web page before they attempt to work the problems.

Selected Answers:

3.

4.

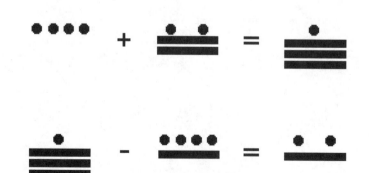

5.

MAYAN MATH

Student Activity Sheet

Name: _____

Date: _____ Per: _____

Mayan Math

1. One country that is sometimes overlooked in the history of mathematics is Mexico. Go to the Web site below and investigate how the Mayans used mathematics. Then answer the questions that follow.

   • http://hanksville.phast.umass.edu/yucatan/mayamath.html

2. Describe the Mayan number system._____

   _____

   _____

   _____

3. Write 19 using Mayan math symbols:

4. Write 4 + 12 and its solution using Mayan math symbols:

5. Write 16 - 9 and its solution using Mayan math symbols:

6. Write out a problem using Mayan math symbols and give it to another student in your class to solve:

WHAT COMES AFTER A BILLION?

Teacher Notes

NCTM Standards, Grades 5–8: Problem Solving, Communication, Reasoning, Connections, Number Relationships, and Computation.

Objectives:

Students will…

- use the Internet to record the current amount of the national debt.

- use the national debt to explore number concepts.

- use the Internet to find out the current U.S. population and then use that information to calculate each person's share of the debt.

- use the Internet to access the national debt amount at different times and then use that information to calculate the percentage of increase for the debt.

- calculate the amount required to be paid each month in order to pay off the debt by the time they graduate from high school.

Materials Needed:

- Computer with Internet access
- Calculator

Web Sites:

- http://www.brillig.com/debt_clock
- http://www.census.gov/
- http://www.yahoo.com/Regional/U_S_States/

Time: approximately 2 hours

Teaching the Lesson:

- This lesson can be used in conjunction with a lesson on budgeting or with a social studies unit exploring the United States government.

- This lesson can also serve as an extension to a lesson on place value and reading and writing numbers.

- The last question that deals with paying off the debt may present some difficulties for students. To simplify the question for students, you can assume that the debt will not increase over the payoff period. Of course, the debt is still increasing, but taking this factor into consideration makes this a very difficult problem.

- Review or introduce the concepts of expanded notation and scientific notation.

WHAT COMES AFTER A BILLION?

Student Activity Sheet

Name: _____

Date: _____ Per: _____

What does come after a billion? Some of you might have answered a billion one, or some of you may have said one trillion. Both answers could be correct, but did you know that one possible answer could have been the national debt? That is right; the national debt is well over one billion. Find out more about the national debt by completing the investigation below.

The National Debt

Visit the Web page below to find out more about the national debt.

The National Debt Clock

- http://www.brillig.com/debt_clock

Define what the national debt represents: _____

_____

_____

_____

_____

1. Record the date and time you visited the National Debt Clock site. _____

2. Record the amount of the national debt. _____

3. Which digit is in the ten billions' place? _____

4. Which digit is in the hundred millions' place? _____

WHAT COMES AFTER A BILLION? *(cont.)*

5. Use words to write out the amount of the national debt.

_____

_____

_____

6. Write the amount of the national debt using expanded notation.

_____

_____

_____

7. Write the national debt using scientific notation. _____

Your Fair Share

The national debt is a lot of money. How much does that mean every person in the United States would have to contribute to pay off the debt? Visit the "U.S. Census Pop Clock" and record the current population estimate.

U.S. Census Bureau Pop Clock

• http://www.census.gov/

1. Record the current U.S. population. _____

2. Based on the national debt amount and the U.S. population, how much is each person's share?

_____

_____

WHAT COMES AFTER A BILLION? *(cont.)*

3. What is the class's share of the national debt?

_____

4. What is the share of the national debt in the state where you live?

Go to the Web page below and record your state's population.

State's Population

- http://www.yahoo.com/Regional/U_S_States/

State Population: _____

My state's share of the national debt: _____

Just How Big Is It Getting?

1. Visit the National Debt Clock each day for the next two days. Record the date and time and amount of the national debt in the table below (the first line should be the amount from your first visit to the debt clock).

2. Calculate the time that has elapsed between each visit in minutes as well as the change in the debt balance.

Date, Time, and Amounts of the National Debt

Date	Time	Time Difference	Debt Amount	Debt Amount Difference

WHAT COMES AFTER A BILLION? *(cont.)*

3. Look over your table and calculate the percentage increase of the national debt for each time you visited the debt clock.

The national debt percentage of increase for each period:

_____

_____

_____

_____

4. Calculate an overall average increase per minute.

_____

_____

_____

Paying Off the Debt

1. Based on the average rate of increase, what will the national debt be when you graduate from high school?

_____

_____

_____

_____

2. If you were the only one paying, how much would you have to pay each month in order to pay off the national debt by the time you graduate from high school?

_____

_____

_____

_____

PLANES

Teacher Notes

NCTM Standards, Grades 5–8: Reasoning, Connections, Number Relationships, Computation, Statistics, and Measurement.

Objectives:

Students will...

- use the Internet to gather information about different types of aircraft.
- determine the most efficient types of aircraft for passenger travel.
- use airline flight schedules from the Internet to determine aircraft speed and distance requirements.
- construct paper airplanes and take measurements to determine their speeds.
- use the information from their paper airplanes to design a flight.

Materials Needed:

- Computer with Internet access
- Masking tape
- Calculators
- Stopwatches
- Tape measures

Web Sites:

- http://www.boeing.com/bck_html/com.html
- http://www.mdc.com/version2/commercial/commercial.htm
- http://www.db.erau.edu/www_virtual_lib/aviation/airlines.html
- http://www.proximus.com/yahoo
- http://www.indo.com/distance
- http://www.compusyst.com/tzone.htm
- http://www.execpc.com/~wallin/convert

Time: approximately 2–3 hours

Teaching the Lesson:

- Many students will not be familiar with the types of airplanes that are commonly used for passenger travel. Help students choose the most common types, such as DC-9, DC-10, 727, 737, 757, 747, 767, etc.
- When students are considering the second question (passenger to range ratio), elicit from them why this might be a consideration when deciding on which airplane to select for which route.
- For step number three, any major airline's flight schedule will work. Reinforce the distance formula and work through an example with them. Be sure to explain time zone changes and what a layover means. You may also choose to disregard daylight savings time.
- When students are constructing their own paper airplanes, any design will work.
- You might want to work through an example conversion from feet per second to miles per hour.

PLANES

Student Activity Sheet

Name: _____

Date: _____ Per: _____

During the course of a day, hundreds of planes land and take off from some of the busiest airports. In order to keep track of all those planes, airports have to stick to a tight schedule, but it is up to the pilots to make sure they get the planes from one airport to another on time. What kinds of information do you think pilots need to know in order to make sure their planes arrive on time? You will have a chance to act as a pilot and help plan an airline schedule that will answer some of those questions. Then, by building your own paper airplane and taking measurements, you will be able to be president of your own airline.

Airplane Characteristics

1. To begin planning your flight schedule, you should learn about some of the characteristics of airplanes that are used for passenger travel. Visit the Web sites below, and for three different types of airplanes, find out the cruising speed, range, and the maximum number of passengers they can carry. Record your findings in the table below.

   • http://www.boeing.com/bck_html/com.html

   • http://www.mdc.com/version2/commercial/commercial.htm

Airplane Type	Cruising Speed	Range	Maximum Number of Passengers

2. Using the information from your table, figure out which plane has the best passenger to range ratio and explain why this might matter to an airline.

_____

_____

_____

PLANES *(cont.)*

Flight Schedules

1. Visit one major airline's Web site and look up its flight schedules. Select at least ten different routes in the continental United States. Notice that airlines give departure times and arrival times. However, they do not tell you how fast the plane will travel or how far you go. Knowing that information is the pilot's job. Luckily, the pilots have you to help them figure all that out. As you select your routes, fill in the table on the next page. In order to calculate the speed at which the plane must travel to arrive on time, you will have to first find out how far you have to go. You will also need to know how long you have to get there. To find out how far cities are from one another, go to one of the Web sites below. Select non-stop flights, or take into account layover times. See the example below to help you. Be sure to account for time zone changes. See the Web page below for time zone boundaries.

For airline flight schedules go to

- http://www.db.erau.edu/www_virtual_lib/aviation/airlines.html

For distances between cities go to

- http://www.proximus.com/yahoo

or

- http://www.indo.com/distance

For time zone boundaries go to

- http://www.compusyst.com/tzone.htm

Example: You have a flight that departs San Diego, CA, at 12:00 P.M., PST

and flies non-stop to Dallas, TX, and arrives at 6:00 P.M., CST.

Time = 4 hours   Distance = 1000 miles

$s = \dfrac{d}{t}$ Let s = speed, d = distance, and t = time.

If d = 1000 miles and t = 4 hours, a plane would have to travel $s = \dfrac{1,000 \text{ miles}}{4 \text{ hours}}$

or 250 mph to arrive on time.

PLANES (cont.)

	City Departing	City Arriving At	Departure Time	Arrival Time	Total Time of Flight	Distance
1.						
2.						
3.						
4.						
5.						
6.						
7.						
8.						
9.						
10.						

PLANES *(cont.)*

2. From what you have learned about aircraft speed and range capabilities, would the airplanes you investigated at the beginning of the lesson be able to meet the speed and distance requirements for each route? Explain.

_____

_____

_____

_____

_____

Build Your Own Airlines

1. Now it is your turn to be president of your own mini paper airline company. First, you have to construct your airplane. You may use any design you want to build your paper airplane. If you are having trouble, seek the expert help of one of your classmates.

2. To set up your airline schedule, conduct an experiment to determine how fast your paper airplane flies. Start by marking off a short distance (10–15 feet or 3–4.5 meters). To help you get more accurate times, have the ending point be a wall. Have one person fly his or her paper airplane while someone else acts as timekeeper. Fly your plane at least five different times. Be sure to record the times in the table below. When you are the timekeeper, record times to the nearest hundredth of a second.

Flight Number	1	2	3	4	5
Time					

3. Figure out the average time it took your paper airplane to fly the distance you measured. Use that information to calculate the speed of your airplane. Remember, your speed should be given as miles per hour, so you will need to convert from feet per second to miles per hour. To help you with the conversion, visit the Web site below. Show your work on the following page.

- http://www.execpc.com/~wallin/convert

PLANES *(cont.)*

Airplanes speed in miles per hour = _____

4. Now you are ready to set up your airline's schedule. Select five cities to use as departure cities and five cities to use as arrival cities. Go to the Web sites from question number one in "Flight Schedules" to find out how far apart your cities are. Pick departure times, and based on the speed of your airplane, record arrival times. Be sure to take into account changes in time zones. Fill in your schedule on the next page.

PLANES *(cont.)*

	City Departing	City Arriving At	Departure Time	Arrival Time	Total Time of Flight	Distance
1.						
2.						
3.						
4.						
5.						
6.						
7.						
8.						
9.						
10.						

TOP SECRET DATA COLLECTION

Teacher Notes

NCTM Standards, Grades 5–8: Problem Solving, Communication, Connections, Number Relationships, Computation, and Statistics.

Objectives:

Students will…

- use the Internet to visit the "Central Intelligence Agency's Factbook" to gather information about countries around the world.

- explore the mathematical connections regarding different aspects of countries, such as communications, population, geography, and economics.

Materials Needed:

- Computer with Internet access

- Calculator

- Protractor

- Compass

Web Site:

- http://www.odci.gov/cia/publications/nsolo/wfb-all.htm

Time: approximately 2 hours

Teaching the Lesson:

- This lesson can be integrated with a social studies or geography lesson that makes comparisons of different countries.

- The "CIA Factbook" Web page is divided into different sections such as regions, transportation, people, economy, and so on. Students need to be careful to access the proper category when gathering information.

- Students will need a lesson on how to construct a circle graph.

- Review mean, median, mode, and range.

TOP SECRET DATA COLLECTION

Student Activity Sheet

Name: _____

Date: _____ Per: _____

Did you know that the Central Intelligence Agency (CIA) does a lot more than just spy on people? A big part of their job is to keep track of all sorts of information about the countries in the world. In fact, the CIA keeps such detailed records they even know how many telephones each country has. As you might have guessed, all those records amount to a lot of numbers, and where there are a lot numbers, there is a good chance that a math investigation follows. So stay tuned.

Communications

Go to the Central Intelligence Agency's Web site below and select any four countries in the world. Fill in the table below.

Central Intelligence Agency's World Factbook

- http://www.odci.gov/cia/publications/nsolo/wfb-all.htm

Population and Numbers of Telephones and Televisions

Country	Population	Number of Telephones	Number of Televisions
(Ex.) United States	266,476,278	183,000,000	215,000,000
1.			
2.			
3.			
4.			

1. For each country, write an inequality (>, <, =) describing the relationship between the population and the number of telephones and the number of televisions.

(Ex.) United States: Population > Number of Televisions > Number of Telephones

TOP SECRET DATA COLLECTION *(cont.)*

2. How many telephones are there per household in each country in your table? Assume four people per household.

_____

_____

3. How many televisions are there per household in each country in your table? Assume four people per household.

_____

_____

4. Collect the per household data for telephones from the entire class. Which country has the most telephones per household? Which country has the least number of telephones per household? Answer the same questions for the number of televisions per household.

_____

_____

People

Select four other countries and record their populations and the three highest ethnic percentages in the table below.

Ethnic Makeup of Population

Country	Population	Race/ Percentage	Race/ Percentage	Race/ Percentage
(Ex.) United States	266,476,278	White/ 83.4%	Black/ 12.4%	Asian/ 3.3%
1.				
2.				
3.				
4.				

TOP SECRET DATA COLLECTION *(cont.)*

1. Based on each country's population and ethnic percentages, calculate how many people comprise each race.

   _____

   _____

   _____

2. If you total the people of all races, do they equal the amount of the entire population? Why or why not?

   _____

   _____

   _____

Geography

Using the "CIA Factbook" Web page, search for the highest point on each continent. Record the locations and heights in the table below.

Highest Point on Each Continent

Continent	Location	Height Meters and Feet
(Ex.) North America	Mount McKinley	6,194 meters 20,321 feet
1.		
2.		
3.		
4.		
5.		
6.		

TOP SECRET DATA COLLECTION *(cont.)*

1. Display the results using a bar graph. Label the y-axis "Height" and label the x-axis "Continent."

2. Calculate the mean, median, mode, and range of the continents' highest points.

Mean:_____   Median:_____

Mode:_____   Range:_____

TOP SECRET DATA COLLECTION *(cont.)*

Economy

Visit the "CIA Factbook" and record the composition of the Gross Domestic Product (GDP) for four different countries in the table below.

GDP Composition

Country	Agriculture	Industry	Services
Ex.) United States	2%	23%	75%
1.			
2.			
3.			
4.			

Construct circle graphs (pie charts) showing each country's GDP composition.

FLAGS OF THE SEA

Teacher Notes

NCTM Standards, Grades 5–8: Problem Solving, Communication, Reasoning, Connections, Number Relationships, Computation, Estimation, Patterns, Probability, Geometry, and Measurement.

Objectives:

Students will…

- use the Internet to investigate the mathematics that can be found in International Marine Signal Flags.

- describe signal flags in equivalent terms using fractions, decimals, and percentages.

- conduct a probability experiment using signal flags.

Materials Needed:

- Computer with Internet access and printer

- Calculator

- Poster paper

- Markers

- Rulers, tape measures

Web Sites:

- International Flags and Pennants   http://www.halcyon.com/zylstra/ham/flags/

- International Marine Signal Flags   http://osprey.erin.gov.au/flags/signal-flags.html

Time: approximately 1–2 hours.

Teaching the Lesson:

- Prior to introducing the lesson, encourage your students to pay attention to the flags they see around them and to think of any connections the flags might have to mathematics.

- If you have access to a color printer, it might be useful to print the International Marine Signal Flags. Otherwise, you can print them out and label the different parts of the flags with the appropriate colors.

FLAGS OF THE SEA

Student Activity Sheet

Name: _____

Date: _____ Per: _____

There are flags everywhere you go. You see them in front of buildings, at stadiums, in classrooms, on ships, in parades, and many other places. Flags are important symbols of identification and means of communication. But why do flags look the way they do? In fact, who decides what a flag looks like? And what role do you think mathematics has played in the design of flags? Learn more about flags and mathematics by investigating the questions below.

International Marine Signal Flags

International Marine Signal Flags are a special set of flags used by ships to communicate with each other. Each flag represents a letter which has a special meaning that sends a message to another ship. Take a look at these flags using one of the Web sites below and then answer the questions that follow.

- International Flags and Pennants   http://www.halcyon.com/zylstra/ham/flags/

or

- International Marine Signal Flags   http://osprey.erin.gov.au/flags/signal-flags.html

1. Examine the signal flags carefully and note the key similarities and differences. Pay particular attention to patterns, similarities, and the arrangement of colors.

For instance, you might describe "H" Hotel and "K" Kilo as similar because they both are

divided in half by their colors. Now you try. _____

_____

_____

_____

_____

_____

_____

_____

FLAGS OF THE SEA *(cont.)*

2. Look at the flags again and try to find all the geometric figures they contain. Name at least four figures. List the figures you found and the name of the flag where you found that figure.

   _____

   _____

   _____

3. What is the most common geometric figure you found in the flags?

   _____

4. Look at the flag for "N" November and count the total number of squares it contains. How many squares did you find? In the space below make a drawing that shows all the squares you found.

Fractions and Flags

1. The flag for "E" Echo could be described using fractions. For instance, Echo is ½ blue and ½ red. Look through the flags and describe the five flags found in the table on the next page in terms of fractions.

2. In the remainder of the table, compare sets of flags using fractions. For instance, the blue portion of "G" Golf ($\frac{1}{6} + \frac{1}{6} + \frac{1}{6} = \frac{3}{6} = \frac{1}{2}$) is equal to the red portion of "H" hotel, ½.

FLAGS OF THE SEA *(cont.)*

Fraction Tables

Flag Name	Fractional Description:
(Ex.) "E" Echo	½ red and ½ blue
1. "D" Delta	
2. "T" Tango	
3. "U" Uniform	
4. "Z" Zulu	
5. "C" Charlie	

Sets of Flags to Compare	Flag Comparison:
(Ex.) "G" Golf and "H" Hotel	The blue portion of Golf $= \frac{1}{6} + \frac{1}{6} + \frac{1}{6} = \frac{3}{6} = \frac{1}{2}$ or one-half of the total flag which is equal to the red portion of Hotel or ½ of the total flag.
Set 1. "C" Charlie and "D" Delta	
Set 2 "L" Lima and "O" Oscar	
Set 3. "T" Tango and "J" Juliett	
Set 4. "Z" Zulu and "E" Echo	

FLAGS OF THE SEA *(cont.)*

Flags: Decimals and Percents

Using the information from your previous fraction tables, complete the tables below by converting the fractional descriptions into decimal and percent equivalents. For example, Echo is ½ blue and ½ red; as a decimal it is 0.5 blue and 0 .5 red; as a percent Echo is 50% blue and 50% red.

Flag Name	Decimal Equivalent	Percentage Equivalent
(Ex.) "E" Echo	0.5 blue and 0.5 red	50% blue and 50% red
1. "D" Delta		
2. "T" Tango		
3. "U" Uniform		
4. "Z" Zulu		
5. "C" Charlie		

Sets of Flags to Compare	Flag Comparison (using decimals and percentages):
Set 1. "C" Charlie and "D" Delta	
Set 2. "L' Lima and "O" Oscar	
Set 3. "T" Tango and "J" Juliett	

FLAGS OF THE SEA (cont.)

More Flag Questions

1. Print out a copy of the "I" India flag. In that flag, what is the ratio of the area of the black circle to the area of the entire flag?

_____

_____

_____

2. What is the area of the yellow portion of the "I" India flag?

_____

_____

_____

3. Print out a copy of the "S" Sierra flag. What is the ratio of the area of the inner blue rectangle to the area of the outside white rectangle? Draw a diagram to support your answer.

_____

FLAGS OF THE SEA *(cont.)*

More Flag Questions *(cont.)*

4. Imagine you could enlarge each flag to the size of a bulletin board and put it on a wall. If you were to throw ten darts, how many times would you expect to hit

the orange in the "O" Oscar flag? Explain.

_____

_____

_____

the blue in the "N" November flag? Explain.

_____

_____

_____

the orange in the "Y" Yankee flag? Explain.

_____

_____

_____

FLAGS OF THE WORLD

Teacher Notes

NCTM Standards, Grades 5–8: Problem Solving, Communication, Reasoning, Connections, Number Relationships, Computation, Estimation, Patterns, Probability, Geometry, and Measurement.

Objectives:

Students will...

- use the Internet to investigate the mathematics contained in flags of the world.

- complete a table of flag characteristics.

Materials Needed:

- Computer with Internet access

- Calculator

- Poster paper

- Markers

- Rulers, tape measures

Web Sites:

- http://flags.cesi.it/dirk/index.htm

- http://thepage.simplenet.com/fly/flag.htm

- http://www.ace.unsw.edu.au/fotw/flags/index.html

Time: approximately 2 hours.

Teaching the Lesson:

- It might be necessary to model additional examples of the similarities among flags.

- Extend the flags of the world grouping exercise by having students find more countries that fit into those groups or by making new groups of countries.

FLAGS OF THE WORLD

Student Activity Sheet

Name: _____

Date: _____ Per: _____

Flags of the World

Every country in the world has its own flag, and every flag has some characteristic that distinguishes it from another country's. Similarities among some flags can be seen, depending on their origin or history. Investigate the similarities of the following groups of flags by visiting one of the Web sites below.

- http://flags.cesi.it/dirk/index.htm

or

- http://thepage.simplenet.com/fly/flag.htm

or

- http://www.ace.unsw.edu.au/fotw/flags/index.html

1. What are the similarities that you notice in the flags of these countries: United Kingdom, Australia, Liberia, British Virgin Islands, Hong Kong, Falkland Islands, New Zealand, and the United States? Note the arrangements of colors, ratios, and patterns.

   _____

   _____

   _____

   _____

2. What are the similarities that you notice in the flags of these countries: France, Italy, Cameroon, Spain, Mexico, Costa Rica, and El Salvador? Note the arrangements of colors, ratios, and patterns.

   _____

   _____

   _____

   _____

FLAGS OF THE WORLD *(cont.)*

3. Why do you think these groups of countries' flags are similar in so many ways? Explain.

_____

_____

_____

4. Examine 15 flags from countries of your choice, and list all the geometric figures you can find.

_____

_____

_____

_____

5. Look at the Japanese flag. How much area (put your answer as equivalent percentage, decimal, and fractional terms) does the red circle take up compared to the entire area of the flag? Draw a diagram to support your answer.

_____

6. Look at the Bangladesh flag. How much area (put your answer as equivalent percentage, decimal, and fractional terms) does the red circle take up compared to the entire area of the flag? Draw a diagram to support your answer.

_____

FLAGS OF THE WORLD *(cont.)*

Flag Characteristics

1. Choose any nine countries and examine their flags. In the table below put a check in the appropriate box or boxes and fill in the required information, showing the characteristics of those flags.

Flag Characteristics

Country	Number of Colors	Horizontal Stripes	Vertical Stripes	Thin Stripes	Thick Stripes	Stars	Graphic or Emblem	Geometric Shape
United States	3	X			X	X		
1.								
2.								
3.								
4.								
5.								
6.								
7.								
8.								
9.								

FLAGS OF THE WORLD *(cont.)*

2. What is the average number of colors found in each flag? Explain.

_____

_____

_____

3. Do more flags have vertical or horizontal stripes? Explain.

_____

_____

_____

4. Review the chart you made. What other conclusions can you make about the designs of flags?

_____

_____

_____

_____

ENLARGING FLAGS

Teacher Notes

NCTM Standards, Grades 5–8: Problem Solving, Communication, Reasoning, Connections, Number Relationships, Computation, Estimation, and Measurement.

Objectives:

Students will...

- use proportional reasoning to enlarge a flag onto poster paper.

- create their own flag designs.

Materials Needed:

- Computer with Internet access

- Calculator

- Poster paper

- Markers

- Rulers, tape measures

Web Sites:

- http://flags.cesi.it/dirk/index.htm

- http://thepage.simplenet.com/fly/flag.htm

- http://www.ace.unsw.edu.au/fotw/flags/index.html

- http://nypl.org/research/chss/spe/art/photo/hinex/empire/about.html

- http://www.usis.usemb.se/usflag/flag.specs.html

Time: approximately 2 hours

Teaching the Lesson:

- The flag enlargement exercise will be difficult for students at first. You may want to model the enlargement process, using a simple geometric figure.

- When students enlarge the United States flag, stress the importance of using accurate measurements and detailed labeling.

ENLARGING FLAGS

Student Activity Sheet

Name: _____

Date: _____ Per: _____

Enlarging a Flag

1. Using one of the Web sites below, select any country and print a picture of its flag. On a piece of poster paper, enlarge the picture of the flag, ensuring that the proportions are exactly the same as the smaller picture. Your enlargement should be at least five times larger than the original picture. When you are finished enlarging your flag, use the space below to explain the process you used to enlarge it.

Flag Web Sites:

- http://flags.cesi.it/dirk/index.htm
- http://thepage.simplenet.com/fly/flag.htm
- http://www.ace.unsw.edu.au/fotw/flags/index.html

_____

_____

_____

_____

_____

2. Maintaining the correct proportions when you are enlarging a flag is challenging. Suppose you had to enlarge a flag to cover a side of the Empire State Building. What would the dimensions of your flag be? Go to the Web site below and find out the measurements of the Empire State Building.

- http://nypl.org/research/chss/spe/art/photo/hinex/empire/about.html

Flag dimensions to cover a side of the Empire State Building:

Flag Length _____   Flag Width_____

ENLARGING FLAGS *(cont.)*

Enlarging the United States Flag

Go to the Web site listed below and use the information to draw a mathematically correct picture of the United States flag in the space below. Your drawing should conform to the actual proportions of the flag. On your drawing be sure to label the different sections and indicate the measurements of each part of the flag.

- http://www.usis.usemb.se/usflag/flag.specs.html

Drawing of United States Flag

ENLARGING FLAGS *(cont.)*

Design Your Own Flag

On a separate piece of paper create your own flag design.

Explain to a friend how you came up with the colors and design of your flag.

_____

_____

_____

_____

_____

_____

HOW BIG IS A WHALE?

Teacher Notes

NCTM Standards, Grades 5–8: Problem Solving, Communication, Reasoning, Connections, Number Relationships, Computation, Estimation, Statistics, Geometry, and Measurement.

Objectives:

Students will…

- use the Internet to make comparisons regarding the sizes of whales.
- investigate the differences in length, weight, area, volume, and speed.
- convert between imperial and metric units.
- write questions based on the information they gather.
- invent a method to measure the volume of a whale.
- use information from the Internet to calculate the time it takes for gray whales to migrate from the Arctic Ocean to Baja California.

Materials Needed:

- Computer with Internet access
- Rope or string
- Centimeter grid paper
- Calculator
- Tape measure

Web Sites:

- http://www.bev.net/education/SeaWorld/baleen_whales/phycharbw.html
- http:// www.bev.net/education/SeaWorld/killer_whale/killerwhales.html
- http://www.ties.k12mn.us/~jnorth/jn95/migrations/students/aboutgray.html
- http://www.execpc.com/~wallin/convert
- http://www.mplik.ru/~sg/transl/index.html (browser must be *Java* capable)
- http://www.edmunds.com/edWeb/trucks/Ford.Trucks/t668.97.html
- http:// www.edmunds.com/edWeb/trucks/Chevrolet.Trucks/t265.97.html

Time: approximately 2–3 hours

Teaching the Lesson:

- You may choose to show a short video or provide some information about whales before introducing the lesson.
- Reinforce the idea of making a comparison to a known object to help in making an estimation of very large objects.
- There are numerous Web sites dealing with whales. You may wish to explore alternate sites.
- If there are enough students in the class, you can go outside and have them stand fingertip to fingertip to demonstrate the arm span calculation.
- For the arm span exercise, break students into groups of four or five.

HOW BIG IS A WHALE? *(cont.)*

Teacher Notes *(cont.)*

- Since whale "heights" are not given, you may need to give additional guidance in transferring the scale drawings to the centimeter grid paper.

- Prior to the lesson, introduce a method to find the volume of an irregularly shaped object.

- Review concepts of area and volume.

Selected Answers:

Whales	Whale Lengths (feet/meters)	Whale Weights (pounds/kilos)
Blue	70/21.3	142,000/64,408
Killer	25/7.6	10,000/4,535
Gray	48/14.6	60,000/27,215

HOW BIG IS A WHALE?

Student Activity Sheet

Name: _____

Date: _____ Per: _____

Spend a few minutes thinking about a whale. When you thought of its size, what did you take into consideration—length, width, weight, or maybe something completely different? Sizes can be compared in a number of different ways, but the one thing in common is that all the comparisons rely on mathematics. This investigation about whales will show you how measurements such as length and weight can be used to make size comparisons.

Length

1. Blue, gray, and killer are the names of three common types of whales. Now think about an object that you are more familiar with, let's say a pickup truck. Do you think those whales are longer or shorter than a pickup truck? Explain.

   _____

   _____

   _____

2. Go to one of the Web sites below, and find out how long each type of whale is when it is fully grown. Then fill in the table on the next page with each measurement. Complete the table by making the necessary conversions. Use the conversion table Web site listed below to check your calculations.

Blue whale information

- http://www.bev.net/education/SeaWorld/baleen_whales/phycharbw.html

Killer whale information

- http:// www.bev.net/education/SeaWorld/killer_whale/killerwhales.html

Gray whale information

- http://www.ties.k12mn.us/~jnorth/jn95/migrations/students/aboutgray.html

Conversion table

- http://www.execpc.com/~wallin/convert

- http://www.mplik.ru/~sg/transl/index.html (browser must be *Java* capable)

HOW BIG IS A WHALE? *(cont.)*

Whale Lengths

Whales	Feet	Yards	Centimeters	Meters
Blue whale				
Gray whale				
Killer whale				

3. Visit the Web sites below to find out the lengths of the pickup trucks. Then list the lengths in the table below.

Ford pickup truck

- http://www.edmunds.com/edWeb/trucks/Ford.Trucks/t668.97.html

Chevrolet pickup truck

- http:// www.edmunds.com/edWeb/trucks/Chevrolet.Trucks/t265.97.html

Pickup Truck Lengths

Pickup Truck	Feet	Yards	Centimeters	Meters
Ford				
Chevrolet				

4. How many pickup trucks would you need to line up bumper to bumper to match the length of a blue whale?

_____

_____

_____

5. How many times longer is a blue whale than a gray whale?

_____

_____

_____

HOW BIG IS A WHALE? *(cont.)*

6. In a group, measure the length of each other's arm span in inches. Calculate the group's average arm span length. Then answer the following question. How many students with their arms extended end to end would it take to equal the length of one blue whale?

Arm Span Measurements (inches)

	1.	2.	3.	4.	5.
Arm Span					

Group's average arm span: _____

Number of students to equal one blue whale: _____

7. Write a question that asks about the length of a whale versus another object, person, or animal. Then give your question to another student and have him or her answer it.

_____

_____

_____

Solve here:

8. Using a piece of string or rope, mark off the length of each type of whale. Experiment to find out how many times you can connect the string or rope across the classroom.

Weight

1. Visit the Web sites you used previously and list the weights for blue, gray, and killer whales in the table below.

HOW BIG IS A WHALE? *(cont.)*

Whale Weights

Whales	Weight (pounds)	Weight (tons)	Weight (grams)	Weight (kilograms)
Blue whale				
Gray whale				
Killer whale				

2. Is the weight of three gray whales greater than, less than, or equal to (>,<,=) the weight of one blue whale? Write an inequality that shows this relationship.

_____

_____

_____

3. If you added the weight of one killer whale, one gray whale, and one blue whale together, would that amount be greater than, less than, or equal to (>,<,=) the combined weights of 10 gray whales? Write an inequality that shows this relationship.

_____

_____

_____

4. Write a question that uses the weights of the different whales to make a comparison. Give it to another student to answer.

_____

_____

_____

Solve here:

HOW BIG IS A WHALE? *(cont.)*

Area

1. Imagine for a moment a whale as a two-dimensional object lying flat on a piece of paper. How could you find the area of that whale? Explain what your procedure would be.

_____

_____

_____

_____

2. Using a piece of centimeter grid paper, make a scale drawing of each type of whale and then calculate its area. List your answers in the table below.

Whale's Area

Whales	Area (inches)	Area (feet)	Area (centimeters)	Area (meters)
Blue whale				
Gray whale				
Killer whale				

3. Measure the area of the floor of your classroom.

Area of Classroom

	Area (inches)	Area (feet)	Area (centimeters)	Area (meters)
Classroom				

HOW BIG IS A WHALE? *(cont.)*

4. How many classroom floors would it take to equal the area of each type of whale?

Blue:_____

Gray: _____

Killer: _____

Volume

1. Suppose you wanted to compare the volumes of the whales. What procedures would you use to try to calculate their volume?

_____

_____

_____

2. Compare your method for finding the volume of a whale with another classmate's and make suggestions that would improve your procedures.

3. Select one of the whales and calculate its volume using the procedure you developed. Then compare your answer with the anwers of the other students who performed the calculation for the same type of whale.

Speed

1. Go to the Web site for the gray whales and find out how fast they swim.

gray whale speed: _____ mph   gray whale speed: _____ k/h

HOW BIG IS A WHALE? *(cont.)*

2. Each year gray whales migrate from the Arctic Circle to Baja California. Use the gray whale Web site and find out how far they travel each year. Then calculate how long (time) the journey takes.

To calculate the time, use the formula time (t) = distance (d) ÷ speed (s) or **t = d ÷ s**.

Distance from Arctic circle to Baja California: _____ miles _____ km

Time

	Hours	Days	Months
Time			

3. Go back to the Web site for the gray whale and find out its life span. What percentage of a gray whale's life is spent migrating back and forth between the Arctic Circle and Baja California?

_____

_____

_____

_____

MATH AROUND THE WORLD

Teacher Notes

NCTM Standards, Grades 5–8: Communication, Connections, and Number Relationships.

Objectives:

Students will...

- use the Internet to investigate the history of mathematics using major geographic regions as a guide.

- construct a time line based on significant mathematical discoveries and the lives of mathematicians.

Materials Needed:

- Computer with Internet access

- Poster board

Web Sites:

- http://aleph0.clark.edu/~djoyce/mathlist/earth.html

- http://www-groups.dcs.st-andrews.ac.uk/~history/

- http://forum.swarthmore.edu/~steve/steve/mathhistory.html

Time: approximately 2 hours

Teaching the Lesson:

- This lesson can be integrated with applicable social studies lessons.

- There are numerous Web pages about the history and people of mathematics. The student activity sheets list several good "jumping off" points for students to begin searching.

- Time lines can be done on a piece of poster paper.

- For the regional research and biography sections, let students work in pairs or small groups.

MATH AROUND THE WORLD

Student Activity Sheet

Name: _____

Date: _____ Per: _____

The history of mathematics is a good example of how ideas can be connected from different cultures and people from all over the world. Mathematics was not invented in one country or by one person. Hundreds of people in many different countries around the world have contributed and continue to make contributions to mathematics. Your investigation of the history of mathematics will take you to many different countries and periods of time. So get set for an adventure. Perhaps someday you will make a lasting contribution to the field of mathematics.

Organize Your Search and Collect Information

1. Using the Web sites listed below, begin studying the history of mathematics by exploring the contributions from different regions around the world. Listed below are some regions where there have been a significant number of mathematical discoveries. As you explore each region, fill in the tables that follow with information about famous mathematicians, time periods, important discoveries, and any other information that you think is significant.

Greece   Europe   Babylon   Asia   India   Africa   Islam

History of Mathematics

- http://aleph0.clark.edu/~djoyce/mathlist/earth.html

MacTutor History

- http://www-groups.dcs.st-andrews.ac.uk/~history/

Math Forum/Math History

- http://forum.swarthmore.edu/~steve/steve/mathhistory.html

MATH AROUND THE WORLD *(cont.)*

Greece

Famous Mathematicians	Time Period	Important Discoveries/Contributions
Other Information		

Asia

Famous Mathematicians	Time Period	Important Discoveries/Contributions
Other Information		

MATH AROUND THE WORLD *(cont.)*

Europe

Famous Mathematicians	Time Period	Important Discoveries/Contributions
Other Information		

Babylon

Famous Mathematicians	Time Period	Important Discoveries/Contributions
Other Information		

MATH AROUND THE WORLD *(cont.)*

India

Famous Mathematicians	Time Period	Important Discoveries/Contributions
Other Information		

Africa

Famous Mathematicians	Time Period	Important Discoveries/Contributions
Other Information		

MATH AROUND THE WORLD *(cont.)*

Islam

Famous Mathematicians	Time Period	Important Discoveries/Contributions
Other Information		

Time Line

Look back over the information you collected in your tables and organize the significant events and mathematicians by year on the time line on the next page. Three time lines are provided because one might not be long enough. If you run out of space on the first time line, continue with the second one and then the third.

MATH AROUND THE WORLD *(cont.)*

Math History Time Line

MATHEMATICIANS

Teacher Notes

NCTM Standards, Grades 5–8: Communication, Connections, and Number Relationships.

Objectives:

Students will…

- use the Internet to make an in-depth study of the biographies of three mathematicians.

- use the Internet to find out which mathematicians have the same birthday as they do.

Materials Needed:

- Computer with Internet access

- Poster board

Web Sites:

- http://aleph0.clark.edu/~djoyce/mathlist/earth.html

- http://www-groups.dcs.st-andrews.ac.uk/~history/

- http://forum.swarthmore.edu/~steve/steve/mathhistory.html

- http://www-groups.dcs.st-and.ac.uk/~history/Day_files/Year.html

- http://dimacs.rutgers.edu/~judyann/calendar/Calendar.html

Time: approximately 2 hours

Teaching the Lesson:

- This lesson can be integrated with applicable social studies lessons.

- There are numerous Web pages about the history and people of mathematics. The student activity sheets list several good "jumping off" points for students to begin searching.

- In-depth biographies can be found on some of the specialized Web pages instead of the broad historical pages.

- For the regional research and biography sections, let students work in pairs or small groups.

MATHEMATICIANS

Student Activity Sheet

Name: _____

Date: _____ Per: _____

Famous Mathematicians

Using the Web sites below as guides, select three famous mathematicians. For each mathematician you select, write a short, one-paragraph biography that includes information about their lives and their important contributions to mathematics. Select mathematicians from as many different backgrounds as you can.

History of Mathematics

- http://aleph0.clark.edu/~djoyce/mathlist/earth.html

MacTutor History

- http://www-groups.dcs.st-andrews.ac.uk/~history/

Math Forum/Math History

- http://forum.swarthmore.edu/~steve/steve/mathhistory.html

1. Name of mathematician: _____

Biography:_____

_____

_____

_____

_____

_____

_____

_____

_____

_____

MATHEMATICIANS *(cont.)*

2. Name of mathematician: _____

Biography:_____

_____

_____

_____

_____

_____

_____

_____

_____

3. Name of mathematician: _____

Biography:_____

_____

_____

_____

_____

_____

_____

_____

_____

MATHEMATICIANS *(cont.)*

A Mathematician's Birthday

1. Go to one of the Web sites below and find a mathematician who was born on the same day as you.

   - Math Birthdayshttp://www-groups.dcs.st-and.ac.uk/~history/Day_files/Year.html
   - Math Birthdayshttp://dimacs.rutgers.edu/~judyann/calendar/Calendar.html

Mathematician's name: _____ Date of birth: _____

2. Describe his or her major contribution to the field of mathematics:_____

   _____

   _____

3. If he or she were still alive, how old would he or she be? _____

   _____

   _____

Design a Birthday Card

On a piece of poster paper, design a birthday card for your mathematician.

FUN WITH MATH WORDS

Teacher Notes

NCTM Standards, Grades 5–8: Problem Solving, Communication, and Connections.

Objectives:

Students will...

- unscramble words and then use the Internet to find their definitions.

- use their math text or math dictionaries found on the Internet to find five words to scramble for their partners to solve.

Materials Needed:

- Computer with Internet access

Web Sites:

- http://www.mathpro.com/math/glossary/glossary.html

- http://www.gps.caltech.edu/~eww/math/math.html

- http://mathcentral.uregina.ca/RR/glossary/middle/

Time: approximately 2 hours

Teaching the Lesson:

- As students find definitions, encourage them to put the definitions in their own words or to provide an example of a problem using that word.

Selected Answers:

Word Scrambles

1. average	2. formula	3. volume	4. ratio	5. equation	6. area
7. triangle	8. measure	9. random	10. probability		

FUN WITH MATH WORDS

Student Activity Sheet

Name: _____

Date: _____ Per: _____

As you have probably noticed, you use a lot of new and unfamiliar words in your math class. Likewise, you have probably noticed that when you understand what all those words mean, it sure makes doing the math a lot easier. Learning what those words mean does not have to be dull and boring. In fact, it can be fun. So, now it is time to begin learning your math vocabulary words the enjoyable way.

Word Scrambles

Below is a list of words you might find in a typical middle school math book. Unscramble the words. Then go to one of the Web sites below and find their definitions.

Math Dictionaries

- http://www.mathpro.com/math/glossary/glossary.html

or

- http://www.gps.caltech.edu/~eww/math/math.html

or

- http://mathcentral.uregina.ca/RR/glossary/middle/

Unscramble these words and write their mathematical definition here:

1. v r e a g a e   _____   _____

   _____

   _____

2. a l m u f r o   _____   _____

   _____

   _____

FUN WITH MATH
WORDS *(cont.)*

3. e l o v m u   _____   _____

_____

4. o r t a i   _____   _____

_____

5. q a t n o i u e   _____   _____

_____

6. r e a a   _____   _____

_____

7. l g t a n e i r   _____   _____

_____

8. s u e m r e a   _____   _____

_____

9. n a d m o r   _____   _____

_____

FUN WITH MATH
WORDS *(cont.)*

10. y i i l t b p o r a b _____   _____

_____

_____

Stump Your Partner

Look through your math book and pick out five words associated with math. Scramble them, and then try to stump your partner or the teacher with your words.

	Scrambled	Unscrambled
1.	_____	_____
2.	_____	_____
3.	_____	_____
4.	_____	_____
5.	_____	_____

MORE FUN WITH MATH WORDS

Teacher Notes

NCTM Standards, Grades 5–8: Problem Solving, Communication, and Connections.

Objectives:

Students will…

- find ten common middle school math terms in the word search table and use the Internet to find their definitions.

- create their own word search table and write two problems using those words.

Materials Needed:

- Computer with Internet access

Web Sites:

- http://www.mathpro.com/math/glossary/glossary.html

- http://www.gps.caltech.edu/~eww/math/math.html

- http://mathcentral.uregina.ca/RR/glossary/middle/

Time: approximately 2 hours

Teaching the Lesson:

- Some students might want to expand the word search they create. One centimeter grid paper works well for this.

- Before students write their word problems, you may need to model how to write word problems.

MORE FUN WITH MATH WORDS (cont.)

Answers to word search:

```
S  W  F  G  Y  U  L  V  T  O  P  S  Q  U  A  R  E  E  W  Q
D  F  E  J  K  L  E  A  R  R  T  Y  N  C  Z  X  I  O  C  P
A  A  T  D  G  N  N  R  Y  R  P  H  A  L  K  D  S  S  I  I
F  V  A  L  G  O  R  I  T  H  M  G  K  L  W  Q  N  B  R  C
L  Y  M  U  I  E  W  A  Q  J  K  D  F  A  H  B  N  U  C  E
D  Y  I  V  B  M  E  B  W  G  H  J  K  Y  E  T  W  S  U  K
A  D  T  Q  L  B  X  L  R  T  T  H  J  K  W  A  G  A  M  N
W  C  S  V  B  N  M  E  R  N  K  U  R  N  F  D  K  N  F  D
K  E  E  C  H  J  W  K  O  P  H  H  D  J  V  M  B  F  E  T
K  V  R  M  F  M  Y  I  T  K  I  H  R  K  T  G  M  B  R  L
W  H  H  G  G  K  S  Y  C  T  N  K  Y  N  V  H  P  P  E  O
I  T  W  F  K  S  F  L  A  O  C  G  L  T  N  O  F  V  N  N
M  U  T  U  E  R  B  M  F  P  R  I  Y  N  F  M  R  N  C  L
R  M  V  R  I  N  B  R  N  R  E  A  S  O  N  A  B  L  E  M
U  R  P  V  M  B  K  T  J  F  A  K  Y  H  T  N  V  B  M  T
E  X  Y  E  B  I  O  P  D  K  S  F  K  H  J  D  T  E  C  C
E  R  H  J  K  D  N  K  V  W  E  M  B  E  U  E  L  F  T  I
```

MORE FUN WITH MATH WORDS

Student Activity Sheet

Name: _____

Date: _____ Per: _____

Word Search

The 10 words listed below are some of the most important mathematical concepts you will study. Go to one of the Web sites below and write out the definition for each word. Then your job is to search for the words in the table on the next page. Keep in mind that the words can be written horizontally, vertically, diagonally, or backwards.

- http://www.mathpro.com/math/glossary/glossary.html

- http://www.gps.caltech.edu/~eww/math/math.html

- http://mathcentral.uregina.ca/RR/glossary/middle/

Find these words: Write their definitions:

1. algorithm: _____

   _____

2. circumference: _____

   _____

3. reasonable: _____

   _____

4. increase: _____

   _____

5. expression: _____

   _____

6. factor: _____

   _____

MORE FUN WITH MATH
WORDS *(cont.)*

7. estimate: _____

_____

8. length: _____

_____

9. square: _____

_____

10. variable: _____

_____

```
S W F G Y U L V T O P S Q U A R E E W Q
D F E J K L E A R R T Y N C Z X I O C P
A A T D G N N R Y R P H A L K D S S I I
F V A L G O R I T H M G K L W Q N B R C
L Y M U I E W A Q J K D F A H B N U C E
D Y I V B M E B W G H J K Y E T W S U K
A D T Q L B X L R T T H J K W A G A M N
W C S V B N M E R N K U R N F D K N F D
K E E C H J W K O P H H D J V M B F E T
K V R M F M Y I T K I H R K T G M B R L
W H H G G K S Y C T N K Y N V H P P E O
I T W F K S F L A O C G L T N O F V N N
M U T U E R B M F P R I Y N F M R N C L
R M V R I N B R N R E A S O N A B L E M
U R P V M B K T J F A K Y T N V B M T
E X Y E B I O P D K S F K H J D T E C C
E R H J K D N K V W E M B E U E L F T I
```

MORE FUN WITH MATH WORDS *(cont.)*

Word Search Challenge

Look through some of the word problems in your math book and select five mathematical words. Use those words to create a word search graph. On the next page, write two problems that are similar in design and strategy to the problems from which you got your words. Make sure you include pictures, tables, and solutions. When you are finished filling in your words and writing your problems, exchange papers with your partner and find each other's words in the table and solve each other's problems.

Search for these words:

1.

2.

3.

4.

5.

MORE FUN WITH MATH WORDS *(cont.)*

Word Search Challenge Problems

Write two word problems that use two of the math concepts you selected for your word search challenge. Give the problems to another student to solve. Check the student's answers.

Problem number one:

_____

_____

_____

_____

_____

_____

_____

_____

_____

Problem number two:

_____

_____

_____

_____

_____

_____

_____

_____

_____

HOW ACCURATE ARE WEATHER FORECASTS?

Teacher Notes

NCTM Standards, Grades 5–8: Connections, Number Relationships, Reasoning, Statistics, and Computation.

Objectives:

Students will...

- use the Internet to select 5 major cities and record forecasted high and low temperatures twice a week over a period of two or four weeks.
- use the Internet to record reported high and low temperatures for the cities they choose.
- evaluate the temperature data to find the mean difference between the forecasted high and low and the reported high and low temperature for each city.
- develop a model to measure the accuracy of weather forecasts.
- display their data and findings on poster paper, using charts, graphs, and tables.

Materials Needed:

- Computer with Internet access
- Calculator
- Poster paper

Web Sites:

- http://www.nationalgeographic.com/ngs/maps/atlas/namerica/usofamm.html
- http://www.lib.utexas.edu/Libs/PCL/Map_collection/Map_collection.html
- http://weather.yahoo.com
- http://www.netcast.noaa.gov/weather.html
- http://www.intellicast.com/cast

Time: approximately 3–4 hours

Teaching the Lesson:

- If necessary, this lesson can be done in a shorter period of time or with fewer temperature observations.
- Ensure that students select "major" cities since getting temperature information for smaller cities is difficult. Also, encourage students to select cities in different geographic locations.
- Forecasts are given for the next day and in some cases for the next several days. You may wish to modify the assignment by evaluating the forecasts for the next 48 or 72 hours.
- When students record the difference between the forecasted high and low and reported high and low temperatures, they need to be recorded as positive numbers regardless of their true difference. This can lead to an interesting discussion regarding absolute value.
- When students are evaluating their data, they will likely find the average high and low temperatures. Stress that they are finding the average difference between the forecasted high and reported high temperatures and likewise for the forecasted and reported and low temperatures.
- As an extension, have the class compile all of their data to build a more accurate model.
- Prior to the lesson review the concepts of average.

HOW ACCURATE ARE WEATHER FORECASTS?

Student Activity Sheet

Name: _____

Date: _____ Per: _____

At one time or another, you have probably noticed that weather forecasts are not always accurate. Wouldn't it be nice to have a better idea of just how accurate and reliable those predictions are? By first observing weather forecasts and then observing the reported temperatures in 5 different cities, you will be able to make a model that tells you just how accurate forecasts really are.

Select Your Cities

1. First, you will need to select 5 "major" cities to keep track of their high and low temperature forecasts. Go to one of the Web sites below and select 5 different major cities, and write their names in the tables on the next pages. Choose cities from different geographic locations.

   - http://www.nationalgeographic.com/ngs/maps/atlas/namerica/usofamm.html

or

   - http://www.lib.utexas.edu/Libs/PCL/Map_collection/Map_collection.html

2. Go to one of the weather Web pages below and record the forecasted high and low temperatures for the cities you chose. Record the temperatures in the tables on the following pages.

   - http://weather.yahoo.com
   - http://www.netcast.noaa.gov/weather.html
   - http://www.intellicast.com/cast
   - http://accuwx.com

3. The next day you will need to go to one of the Web sites below and record the actual reported high and low temperatures for all 5 of your cities. Find the differences between the forecasted and actual temperatures. You will repeat this process twice a week for two weeks. For example, first log on Monday and record the forecasted high and low temperatures for Tuesday. Log on again Wednesday to get the actual temperatures and the forecast for Thursday. Friday, log on again and record the actual temperatures for Thursday.

   - http://www.iwin.nws.noaa.gov/iwin/world.html
   - http://www.nssl.uoknor.edu/~nws/wx.html

HOW ACCURATE ARE WEATHER FORECASTS? *(cont.)*

4. After you record your reported high and low temperatures, find the differences between the forecast temperatures and the reported temperatures.

City Name					
	1	2	3	4	5
Date					
Forecast High					
Reported High					
Difference					
Forecast Low					
Reported Low					
Difference					

City Name					
	1	2	3	4	5
Date					
Forecast High					
Reported High					
Difference					
Forecast Low					
Reported Low					
Difference					

HOW ACCURATE ARE WEATHER FORECASTS? *(cont.)*

City Name					
	1	2	3	4	5
Date					
Forecast High					
Reported High					
Difference					
Forecast Low					
Reported Low					
Difference					

City Name					
	1	2	3	4	5
Date					
Forecast High					
Reported High					
Difference					
Forecast Low					
Reported Low					
Difference					

HOW ACCURATE ARE WEATHER FORECASTS? *(cont.)*

City Name					
	1	2	3	4	5
Date					
Forecast High					
Reported High					
Difference					
Forecast Low					
Reported Low					
Difference					

What Is the Difference?

Once you have recorded all your data, calculate the average temperature differences for the highs and lows for each of your 5 cities.

City Name					
	1	2	3	4	5
Mean Difference—High					
Mean Difference—Low					

HOW ACCURATE ARE WEATHER FORECASTS? *(cont.)*

Use the data from the table you built to calculate the average difference for the high and low temperatures for all 5 cities combined.

1. Average difference between forecast and reported high temperatures: _____

2. Average difference between forecast and reported low temperatures: _____

Summary

1. Based on your observations and the evaluation of your data, how accurate are weather forecasts? Explain.

   _____

   _____

   _____

2. Would you come to a different conclusion if you conducted this experiment during a different time of the year? Why or why not?

   _____

   _____

   _____

   _____

HOW ACCURATE ARE WEATHER FORECASTS? *(cont.)*

3. Which city had the most accurate weather forecasts?

   _____

4. Which city had the least accurate weather forecasts?

   _____

5. Why were some cities' forecasts more accurate than others?

   _____

   _____

   _____

Displaying Your Results

Organize your data on poster paper by creating a chart, graph, or table. Try to make the data visually interesting, remember to label your table and graphs, and use appropriate legends. You may want to use a computer graphing program to help you.

A PENNY FOR YOUR THOUGHTS

Teacher Notes

NCTM Standards, Grades 5–8: Problem Solving, Reasoning, Connections, Number Relationships, Computation, Statistics, Geometry, and Measurement.

Objectives:

Students will…

- measure the diameter of several different types of coins and use the information to calculate area and circumference.
- use the Internet to find the actual diameter of each type of coin and determine the level of accuracy of their measurements.
- weigh each type of coin and make conversions between metric and imperial units.
- use the Internet to find the actual weight of each type of coin.
- measure the height of each type of coin and use that information to solve problems.

Materials Needed:

- Computer with Internet access
- Calculator
- Gram scale
- Ruler or caliper

Web Sites:

- http://www.ustreas.gov/treasury/bureaus/mint/subintro.html
- http://atlantis.austin.apple.com/people.pages/bcreighton/CoinSpecs.html
- http:// http://www.execpc.com/~wallin/convert
- http://www.mplik.ru/~sg/transl/index.html (browser must be *Java* capable)
- http://www.edmunds.com

Time: approximately 2 hours

Teaching the Lesson:

- You can borrow the scales and possibly the calipers from science teachers at the school.
- When students are measuring the diameter using a ruler, they may have difficulty obtaining a level of accuracy to hundredths of an inch. It is recommended that you have them use calipers instead.
- Errors may result in measuring the diameter because students may be measuring chords instead of diameters. This is a good opportunity to introduce or review the concept of chords and diameters.
- Stress accuracy when students are weighing the coins. If small enough weights are not available, weigh several of the same type of coin at once.

A PENNY FOR YOUR THOUGHTS *(cont.)*

Teacher Notes

Selected Answers:

Coin	Diameter (inches)	Weight (grams)
Penny	0.750	2.5
Nickel	0.835	5
Dime	0.705	2.268
Quarter	0.955	5.67

A PENNY FOR YOUR THOUGHTS

Student Activity Sheet

Name: _____

Date: _____ Per: _____

Coins are pretty amazing. Think about it; you give someone a round piece of metal, and they give you stuff. In other words, coins have value. But they only have value if they meet stringent measurements. Learn more about coin specifications by completing the investigation below.

Area of a Coin

Use a ruler or caliper to measure the diameter of a penny, nickel, dime, and quarter to the nearest hundredth of an inch. Calculate the area of one side of each coin and its circumference. Fill in the table with your results.

Area = $\prod \cdot r^2$ Circumference = $2 \cdot \prod \cdot r$ **or** $d \cdot \prod$

let $\prod$ = 22/7

Area and Circumference of Coins in Inches

Coin	Diameter (in.)	Radius (in.)	Area (sq. in.)	Circumference (in.)
Penny				
Nickel				
Dime				
Quarter				

1. Write an equation that shows the mathematical relationship between the diameter and the radius of each coin.

   _____

   _____

2. For each type of coin, what is the ratio of the circumference to the diameter?

   _____

A PENNY FOR YOUR THOUGHTS *(cont.)*

3. What did you discover about the ratios in problem number two?

_____

_____

_____

How Accurate Are Your Measurements?

Verify the level of precision you obtained with your measurements by visiting one of the Web sites below and recording the exact specifications for the diameter of each type of coin in the table.

United States Mint

- http://www.ustreas.gov/treasury/bureaus/mint/subintro.html

or

- http://atlantis.austin.apple.com/people.pages/bcreighton/CoinSpecs.html

Coin Specifications Comparison

Coin	Actual Diameter (in.)	Measured Diameter (in.)	Difference (in.)
Penny			
Nickel			
Dime			
Quarter			

Were your measurements accurate? Explain.

_____

_____

A PENNY FOR YOUR THOUGHTS *(cont.)*

A Weighty Issue

Use a scale to measure the weight of each type of coin to the nearest hundredth of a gram. Record the weight in grams. Then convert the weight to kilograms, ounces, and pounds and record those weights in the table below. To help you in making the conversions, visit one of the conversion Web sites listed.

Conversion Web Sites

- http:// http://www.execpc.com/~wallin/convert

or

- http://www.mplik.ru/~sg/transl/index.html (browser must be *Java* capable)

Coin Weights

Coin	Grams	Kilograms	Ounces	Pounds
Penny				
Nickel				
Dime				
Quarter				

1. You know that the monetary value of two dimes and a nickel equals a quarter. But what about their weights? Is the weight of two dimes and a nickel greater than, less than, or equal to (>, <, =) the weight of a quarter? Write an inequality describing your answer.

_____

_____

_____

2. How much money would 25 kilograms of nickels equal?

_____

_____

A PENNY FOR YOUR THOUGHTS *(cont.)*

3. How many pounds of quarters would it take to buy your favorite car? To find out how much your favorite car costs, visit the Web site below.

Car Prices

- http://www.edmunds.com

Price, make, and model of your favorite car: _____

Calculate here:

_____ pounds of quarters are needed to buy my car.

Visit one of the coin Web sites and record the actual weights for each coin.

Coin Weights Comparison

Coin	Measured Weight (g)	Actual Weight (g)	Difference
Penny			
Nickel			
Dime			
Quarter			

A PENNY FOR YOUR THOUGHTS *(cont.)*

4. When you measured the different types of coins, which coin had the largest measurement error?

_____

_____

_____

5. Explain how you might have weighed the coins to obtain a greater degree of accuracy.

_____

_____

_____

Height

Measure the height (to the nearest hundredth of an inch) of each coin and record the results in the table.

Coin Heights

Coin	Penny	Nickel	Dime	Quarter
Height (in.)				

1. How high would 100 dollars in dimes be?

_____

_____

2. What would your height be worth in quarters?

_____

_____

MUSIC CHARTS

Teacher Notes

NCTM Standards, Grades 5–8: Problem Solving, Communication, Reasoning, Connections, Number Relationships, Computation, and Statistics.

Objectives:

Students will…

- use the Internet to find out the current "number one" songs in three different categories.

- design a survey to find out how the students in the school compare their favorite songs to the music charts.

- conduct the survey and analyze the data from the survey.

- present their findings.

Materials Needed:

- Computer with Internet access

- Calculator

- Poster paper

Web Sites:

- http://www.billboard-online.com

- http://mtv.com/music/top20/page_three.html

Time: Approximatey 2–3 hours.

Teaching the Lesson:

- This lesson can be used during an election when polls are quite common. It can also be used in conjunction with a social studies unit on polling.

- Provide students with background information about sampling. Many students are not aware of the importance of choosing whom to poll.

- Students will conduct the poll outside of class. Stress that they are to ask only students and should not survey anyone outside of school.

- To ensure that quality data is received, you may want to collect all the potential questions from the students and select the best ones prior to the final design of the survey.

- Prior to the lesson you may want to advise parents that you will be using material from the MTV Web site. Although the material found on the Web page is not necessarily objectionable, some parents may wish that their sons or daughters not have access to it.

MUSIC CHARTS

Student Activity Sheet

Name: _____

Date: _____ Per: _____

Which Song Is Number One?

It sounds like an easy question, but it really depends on who you ask. For instance, if you asked the teachers in the school, their answers would be a lot different than if you asked other students. There is a lot more to polls than just asking questions. Find out how polls really work by completing the investigation that follows.

The Most Popular Song and Album

1. Go to the Web site below. Using the tables provided in this activity, record the top 10 songs and the top 10 albums.

Billboard Music Charts

- http://www.billboard-online.com

2. Next, go to the Web page below. Use the table provided in this activity to record the top 10 music videos.

MTV Top Music Videos

- http://mtv.com/music/top20/page_three.html

Design a School Survey

Now that you know what the most popular songs, albums, and music videos are, you can design a survey to find out how the favorites of the students at your school compare to the top 10.

MUSIC CHARTS *(cont.)*

1. To design this survey you will need to ask questions that will tell you what each respondent's favorite song, album, and music video are. Furthermore, as a part of your survey, you will need to find out some of the characteristics of your respondents, such as gender, age, and grade level. So that you do not influence the choices of the participants, do not indicate in the survey which songs are currently number one. One strategy might be to list the top 10 in random order and have them circle their favorites in each category. Or, just leave it up to them to write in their favorites and do not give them a list.

2. In the space below write some questions that you might use in your survey.

_____

_____

_____

_____

_____

_____

_____

_____

_____

_____

_____

_____

Conduct Your Survey and Tally the Results

1. Once you have written your questions and had them approved by your teacher, conduct your survey. Survey as many students as possible; be sure to include students of different grades and ages.

2. When you have finished conducting the survey, use the tables to tally the results.

Most Popular Single and Characteristics of Respondents

Song List of Responses	Total Number	Male	Female	Age 12	Age 13	Age 14	Grade 6	Grade 7	Grade 8
(ex.) song xyz	IIIII II (7)	III	IIII	II	III	II	II	III	II
1.									
2.									
3.									
4.									
5.									
6.									
7.									
8.									
9.									
10.									
Totals									

MUSIC CHARTS *(cont.)*

Most Popular Albums and Characteristics of Respondents

Album List of Responses	Total Number	Male	Female	Age 12	Age 13	Age 14	Grade 6	Grade 7	Grade 8
(ex.) album title	IIIII II (7)	III	IIII	II	III	II	II	III	II
1.									
2.									
3.									
4.									
5.									
6.									
7.									
8.									
9.									
10.									
Totals									

MUSIC CHARTS *(cont.)*

Most Popular Music Video and Characteristics of Respondents

Music Video List of Responses	Total Number	Male	Female	Age 12	Age 13	Age 14	Grade 6	Grade 7	Grade 8
(ex.) song title	IIIII II (7)	III	IIII	II	III	II	II	III	II
1.									
2.									
3.									
4.									
5.									
6.									
7.									
8.									
9.									
10.									
Totals									

MUSIC CHARTS *(cont.)*

Evaluating Your Results

1. Did the male and female students select the same favorite songs, albums, and music videos? Explain how you were able to determine this.

_____

_____

_____

2. What is the average age of the respondents in your survey?

_____

_____

_____

3. What is the average grade level of the respondents in your survey?

_____

_____

_____

4. How did the results from the survey you conducted compare to the Billboard and MTV charts? Explain.

_____

_____

_____

_____

_____

5. On a separate piece of paper, display the data from your survey.

SALARIES: HOW MUCH DO PROFESSIONAL BASEBALL PLAYERS MAKE?

Teacher Notes

NCTM Standards, Grades 5–8: Problem Solving, Communication, Reasoning, Number Relationships, Computation, Estimation, and Statistics.

Objectives:

Students will…

- use the Internet to investigate the salaries of professional baseball players.
- calculate how much the five highest paid players in baseball earn for one game and for one minute of playing time.
- use the Internet to make further investigations related to the athletes' performances and their salaries.

Materials Needed:

- Computer with Internet access
- Calculator

Web Sites:

- http://www.sjmercury.com/sports/baseball/salaries.htm
- http://bizsports.com/sports/mlb.html
- http://espn.sportszone.com/mlb/
- http://www.majorleaguebaseball.com

Time: 1–2 hours

Teaching the Lesson:

- The intent of the lesson is not to glamorize the salaries of professional athletes but rather to demonstrate how inflated they are. As an extension to the lesson you might want to investigate the probability of becoming a highly paid professional athlete.
- Students may have favorite athletes in professional baseball. If so, you can tailor the lesson so that students investigate their favorite athletes.
- Since salaries fluctuate so frequently, prior to the lesson you may want to conduct a search to find the most current salaries.
- The salaries of top athletes are very high. You can help students gain perspective by having them survey salaries of more common professions.
- As you begin the lesson, model how you would calculate per game and per minute amounts. Stress rounding and estimation.
- Students should not choose pitchers for this investigation.

SALARIES: HOW MUCH DO PROFESSIONAL BASEBALL PLAYERS MAKE?

Student Activity Sheet

Name: _____

Date: _____ Per: _____

How much do professional athletes really make? That is a good question. It seems as if every day you hear about a professional athlete signing a contract worth millions of dollars. It is hard to imagine, let alone understand, just what all that money means. But if you examine the salaries in detail, you can start to make sense of just what those enormous salaries amount to. Explore the connections among salaries, mathematics, and sports by working through the exercises below.

Major League Baseball (MLB)

Go to the Web site below which lists the salaries of major league baseball players and answer the questions that follow.

- http://www.sjmercury.com/sports/baseball/salaries.htm

or

- http://bizsports.com/sports/mlb.html

1. In the table below, list the names of the five highest paid players in baseball (or your five favorite players), not including pitchers, and calculate how much they make for each game of a season. There are 162 games in a season.

MLB Per Game Salary

Player's Name	Yearly Salary	Amount Per Game

SALARIES: HOW MUCH DO PROFESSIONAL BASEBALL PLAYERS MAKE? *(cont.)*

2. Further investigate the players' salaries by calculating how much each of the players makes for each inning in a game. There are nine innings in a baseball game.

MLB Salary Per Inning

Player's Name	Amount Per Game	Amount Per Inning

3. Go to one of the Web sites below to find out how many at-bats each of the players had last year. Estimate how much each of the top five players will make for each at-bat this year. Then calculate the actual figure based on the number of at-bats the player had last year.

- ESPN baseball   http://espn.sportszone.com/mlb/

or

- Major League Baseball   http://www.majorleaguebaseball.com

MLB Amount Per At-Bat

Player's Name	Annual Salary	number of At-Bats Last Year	Estimate Per At-Bat This Year

SALARIES: HOW MUCH DO PROFESSIONAL BASEBALL PLAYERS MAKE? *(cont.)*

4. Although baseball games are not timed, records of each game's length are kept. It has been found that a typical game lasts about three hours. Calculate how much each of the players makes per minute.

MLB Amount Per Minute

Player's Name	Amount Per Game	Amount Per Minute

SALARIES: HOW MUCH DO PROFESSIONAL BASKETBALL PLAYERS MAKE?

Teacher Notes

NCTM Standards, Grades 5–8: Problem Solving, Communication, Reasoning, Number Relationships, Computation, Estimation, and Statistics.

Objectives:

Students will…

- use the Internet to investigate the salaries of professional basketball players.
- calculate how much the five highest paid players in basketball earn for one game and for one minute of playing time.
- use the Internet to make further investigations related to the athletes' performances and their salaries.

Materials Needed:

- Computer with Internet access
- Calculator

Web Sites:

- http://www.chron.com/content/chron…s/bk/bkn/96/11/17/nbasalaries.html
- http://www.bizsports.com/sports/nba.html
- http://espn.sportszone.com/nba/index.html
- http://www.nba.com

Time: 1–2 hours

Teaching the Lesson:

- The intent of the lesson is not to glamorize the salaries of professional athletes but rather to demonstrate how inflated they are. As an extension to the lesson you might want to investigate the probability of becoming a highly paid professional athlete.
- Students may have favorite athletes in professional basketball. If so, you can tailor the lesson so that students investigate their favorite athletes.
- Since salaries fluctuate so frequently, prior to the lesson you may want to conduct a search to find the most current salaries.
- The salaries of top athletes are very high. You can help students gain perspective by having them survey more common salaries.
- As you begin the lesson, model how you would calculate per game and per minute amounts. Stress rounding and estimation.

SALARIES: HOW MUCH DO PROFESSIONAL BASKETBALL PLAYERS MAKE?

Student Activity Sheet

Name: _____

Date: _____ Per: _____

How much do professional athletes really make? That is a good question. It seems as if every day you hear about a professional athlete signing a contract worth millions of dollars. It is hard to imagine, let alone understand, just what all that money means. But if you examine the salaries in detail, you can start to make sense of just what those enormous salaries amount to. Explore the connections among salaries, mathematics, and sports by working through the exercises below.

National Basketball Association (NBA)

Go to one of the Web sites below and find out how much the five highest paid basketball players (or your favorite players) in the NBA make. Then answer the questions that follow.

- http://www.chron.com/content/chron…s/bk/bkn/96/11/17/nbasalaries.html

or

- http://www.bizsports.com/sports/nba.html

1. How much do the players make per game? There are 82 games in an NBA season.

NBA Per Game Salary

Player's Name	Yearly Salary	Amount Per Game

SALARIES: HOW MUCH DO PROFESSIONAL BASKETBALL PLAYERS MAKE? *(cont.)*

2. Using one of the Web sites below, find out the scoring averages per game for the five players. Then calculate their pay per point scored.

- http://espn.sportszone.com/nba/index.html

or

- http://www.nba.com

or

- http://sports.yahoo.com/nba/

NBA Scoring Average Per Game

Player's Name	Scoring Average	Yearly Salary	Amount Per Point

3. Calculate how much the five players make per minute. There are 45 minutes in a basketball game.

NBA Amount Per Minute

Player's Name	Amount Per Game	Amount Per Minute

SALARIES: HOW MUCH DO PROFESSIONAL HOCKEY PLAYERS MAKE?

Teacher Notes

NCTM Standards, Grades 5–8: Problem Solving, Communication, Reasoning, Number Relationships, Computation, Estimation, and Statistics.

Objectives:

Students will…

- use the Internet to investigate the salaries of professional hockey players.
- calculate how much the top five paid athletes in hockey earn for one game and for one minute of playing time.
- use the Internet to make further investigations related to the athletes' performances and their salaries.

Materials Needed:

- Computer with Internet access
- Calculator

Web Sites:

- http://www.canadas.net/Sportif/extra/1997/salary.html
- http://www.travel-finder.com/convert/convert.htm
- http://www.oanda.com (go to 164 currencies converter)
- http://www.nhl.com
- http://espn.sportszone.com/nhl/index.html

Time: 1–2 hours

Teaching the Lesson:

- The intent of the lesson is not to glamorize the salaries of professional athletes but rather to demonstrate how inflated they are. As an extension to the lesson you might want to investigate the probability of becoming a highly paid professional athlete.
- Students may have favorite athletes in professional hockey. If so, you can tailor the lesson so that students investigate their favorite athletes.
- Since salaries fluctuate so frequently, prior to the lesson you may want to conduct a search to find the most current salaries.
- The salaries of top athletes are very high. You can help students gain perspective by having them survey more common salaries.
- As you begin the lesson, model how you would calculate per game and per minute amounts. Stress rounding and estimation.

SALARIES: HOW MUCH DO PROFESSIONAL HOCKEY PLAYERS MAKE?

Student Activity Sheet

Name: _____

Date: _____ Per: _____

How much do professional athletes really make? That is a good question. It seems as if every day you hear about a professional athlete signing a contract worth millions of dollars. It is hard to imagine, let alone understand, just what all that money means. But if you examine the salaries in detail, you can start to make sense of just what those enormous salaries amount to. Explore the connections among salaries, mathematics, and sports by working through the exercises below.

National Hockey League (NHL)

1. Go to the Web site below and list the names and salaries of the five highest paid players (or your favorite five players) in the National Hockey League (NHL). Calculate how much each of those players makes per game. There are 82 games in a NHL season.

   • http://www.canadas.net/Sportif/extra/1997/salary.html

NHL Per Game Salary

Player's Name	Yearly Salary	Amount Per Game

SALARIES: HOW MUCH DO PROFESSIONAL HOCKEY PLAYERS MAKE? *(cont.)*

2. For the five players in the NHL, go to one of the Web sites below to find out how many goals each player scored. Then calculate their salaries per goal scored.

- http://www.nhl.com
- http://sports.yahoo.com/nhl/
- http://espn.sportszone.com/nhl/index.html

NHL Amount Per Goal

Player's Name	number of Goals Scored	Amount Per Goal

3. Calculate how much the NHL players make per minute. There are 60 minutes in a hockey game.

NHL Amount Per Minute

Player's Name	Amount Per Game	Amount Per Minute

SALARIES: HOW MUCH DO PROFESSIONAL HOCKEY PLAYERS MAKE? *(cont.)*

Some of the players in the NHL are paid in Canadian dollars. Select the five highest paid players who are paid in Canadian dollars and record their names and salaries, using one of the currency converters found at one of the Web sites below. Then figure out how much their salaries are equal to in United States dollars. Use the current exchange rate.

- http://www.travel-finder.com/convert/convert.htm

or

- http://www.oanda.com (go to 164 currencies converter)

NHL Salaries: Canadian vs. U.S. Dollars

Player's Name	Canadian Dollars	United States Dollars

SALARIES: HOW MUCH DO PROFESSIONAL FOOTBALL PLAYERS MAKE?

Teacher Notes

NCTM Standards, Grades 5–8: Problem Solving, Communication, Reasoning, Number Relationships, Computation, Estimation, and Statistics.

Objectives:

Students will…

- use the Internet to investigate the salaries of professional football players.
- calculate how much the top five paid athletes in football earn for one game and for one minute of playing time.
- use the Internet to make further investigations related to the athletes' performances and their salaries.

Materials Needed:

- Computer with Internet access
- Calculator

Web Sites:

- http://www.sportsline.com/u/sports…ml/football/LGNS/FBP-SALARY.HTM
- http://espn.sportszone.com/nfl/index.html
- http://sports.yahoo.com/nfl/
- http://www.nfl.com

Time: 1–2 hours

Teaching the Lesson:

- The intent of the lesson is not to glamorize the salaries of professional athletes but rather to demonstrate how inflated they are. As an extension to the lesson you might want to investigate the probability of becoming a highly paid professional athlete.
- Students may have favorite football players. If so, you can tailor the lesson so that students investigate their favorite athletes.
- Since salaries fluctuate so frequently, prior to the lesson you may want to conduct a search to find the most current salaries.
- The salaries of top athletes are very high. You can help students gain perspective by having them survey more common salaries.
- As you begin the lesson, model how you would calculate per game and per minute amounts. Stress rounding and estimation.

SALARIES: HOW MUCH DO PROFESSIONAL FOOTBALL PLAYERS MAKE?

Student Activity Sheet

Name: _____

Date: _____ Per: _____

How much do professional athletes really make? That is a good question. It seems as if every day you hear about a professional athlete signing a contract worth millions of dollars. It is hard to imagine, let alone understand, just what all that money means. But if you examine the salaries in detail, you can start to make sense of just what those enormous salaries amount to. Explore the connections among salaries, mathematics, and sports by working through the exercises below.

National Football League (NFL)

1. Go to the Web site below and list the names and salaries of the highest paid players (or your five favorite players) in the National Football League. Then calculate how much they make per game. There are 16 games in the NFL season.

   • http://www.sportsline.com/u/sports…ml/football/LGNS/FBP-SALARY.HTM

NFL Per Game Salary

Player's Name	Yearly Salary	Amount Per Game

SALARIES: HOW MUCH DO PROFESSIONAL FOOTBALL PLAYERS MAKE? *(cont.)*

2. Calculate how much each of the five NFL players makes per minute. There are 60 minutes in a professional football game.

NFL Amount Per Minute

Player's Name	Amount Per Game	Amount Per Minute

3. Use one of the Web sites below to find the top five point scorers in the NFL last year. Once you find that information, go back to the NFL salary list and calculate how much each player is paid per point scored.

- http://espn.sportszone.com/nfl/index.html

or

- http://sports.yahoo.com/nfl/

or

- http://www.nfl.com

NFL Amount Per Point

Player's Name	Total Points Scored	Yearly Salary	Amount Per Point

SALARY SUMMARY: HOW MUCH DO PROFESSIONAL ATHLETES MAKE?

Teacher Notes

NCTM Standards, Grades 5–8: Problem Solving, Communication, Reasoning, Number Relationships, Computation, Estimation, and Statistics.

Objectives:

Students will…

- use information from previous lessons on sports and make statistical comparisons.

- calculate the average salary for each sport and construct a histogram to make comparisons of salaries per game and per minute.

Materials Needed:

- Computer with Internet access

- Calculator

Web Sites:

Use Web sites from previous lessons.

Time: 1–2 hours

Teaching the Lesson:

- Be careful to calculate the averages of the top five athletes, not an average for the entire sport.

- Students may need help choosing appropriate scales for their graphs.

- Require students to demonstrate how they arrived at their answers.

SALARY SUMMARY: HOW MUCH DO PROFESSIONAL ATHLETES MAKE?

Student Activity Sheet

Name: _____

Date: _____ Per: _____

Salary Comparisons

Now that you have investigated the salaries of the five highest paid players (or your favorite players) in four major professional sports, it is time to compare salaries among the different sports.

1. Go back to the previous sport salary lessons and calculate the average pay of the five players per game for each of the four sports.

Average MLB pay per game: _____

Average NBA pay per game: _____

Average NFL pay per game: _____

Average NHL pay per game: _____

2. When you finish calculating the average pay per game, display the data using a histogram in the space provided on the next page. Be sure to use appropriate scales and label your graph.

SALARY SUMMARY: HOW MUCH DO PROFESSIONAL ATHLETES MAKE? *(cont.)*

**Histogram of Average Pay Per Game of Five Highest Paid Players
for MLB, NBA, NFL, and NHL**

3. Calculate the average pay of the five players per minute for each of the four sports.

Average MLB pay per minute: _____

Average NBA pay per minute: _____

Average NFL pay per minute: _____

Average NHL pay per minute: _____

4. When you finish calculating the average pay per minute, display the data using a histogram in the space provided on the next page. Be sure to use appropriate scales and label your graph.

SALARY SUMMARY: HOW MUCH DO PROFESSIONAL ATHLETES MAKE? *(cont.)*

**Histogram of Average Pay Per Minute of Five Highest Paid Players
for MLB, NBA, NFL, and NHL**

5. Another way to compare the players' salaries is to look at the total number of minutes they play in a season. Using the information you obtained previously, calculate how many minutes there are in an entire season for each of the four sports. Display your data using a histogram in the space provided.

Total Number of Minutes in a Season:

MLB:_____   NBA:_____

NFL:_____   NHL:_____